Problems Presented by Alcoholic Clients

Problems Presented by Alcoholic Clients

A Handbook of Counseling Strategies

by MICHAEL R. JACOBS, PhD

ADDICTION RESEARCH FOUNDATION

Toronto

The views expressed and positions taken in this book are those of the author and do not necessarily represent the views or positions of the Addiction Research Foundation.

No part of this book may be reproduced in any form — except for a brief quotation (not to exceed 1,000 words) in a review or professional work — without the permission in writing from the publisher.

Canadian Cataloguing in Publication Data

Jacobs, Michael R.
  Problems presented by alcoholic clients

Bibliography: p.
ISBN 0-88868-050-3

  1. Alcoholism counseling.   2. Alcoholics —
Rehabilitation.   I. Addiction Research Foundation of Ontario.   II. Title.

HV5276.J32   362.2'9286   C82-094269-3

To June Judith Jacobs

About the Author

After receiving his doctorate in clinical psychology from Ohio's Case Western Reserve University in 1968, Michael Jacobs served as a clinical postdoctoral fellow under the supervision of the president of the American Psychological Association, George Albee. Later, he was chief examiner for the Civil Service Commission in Cleveland, Ohio, and was then invited to organize and direct a Crisis Intervention Unit at Toronto East General Hospital in Toronto, Ontario. Dr. Jacobs joined the Addiction Research Foundation in 1974 as the senior clinician at the Central Toronto Centre. He is currently senior clinical and science writer in the Foundation's Education Resources Division.

Contents

Preface   viii

Acknowledgments   x

Introduction   1

Section

1. Denial   9
2. Continued Drinking while in Treatment   13
3. Relapse   19
4. Motivation   25
5. Inconsistent Attendance   31
6. Mistrust   35
7. Counselor's Hostility towards Clients   39
8. Clients' Hostility towards the Counselor   43
9. Overt but Diffuse Anger   55
10. Serious Psychopathology   59
11. Blaming   63
12. Frequent Lateness for Appointments   67
13. Frequent Telephone Calls when Drinking or Distressed   71
14. Clients Arriving Drunk for Counseling   75
15. Intoxication Suspected   79
16. Refusal to Take Medication   81
17. Game Playing   85
18. Verbally Threatening Behavior when Sober   95
19. Suicidal Tendency   97
20. Age, Sex, and Professional Status of the Counselor   101
21. Social Class and Culture   107
22. Wife's Vested Interest in Client's Alcoholism   117

References   125

Preface

It is generally agreed among mental health workers that alcoholics present more problems than do other types of clients seeking treatment, that they usually do not respond well to counseling, and as a result are unlikely to change their drinking behavior.

Clearly, those assumptions are inseparable. Clients who disrupt the counseling process through continued drinking while in treatment, inconsistent attendance, and other counterproductive behaviors, or who manifest inappropriate motivation and manipulative "game playing" can hardly be viewed with a favorable prognosis.

However, the emphasis of traditional alcoholism counseling may also be at issue. Clients are usually expected to modify their behavior to meet the counselor's expectations. If they do not, they are viewed as uncooperative, unmotivated, manipulative, and so on. While such descriptions may be apt, they are hardly helpful in a search for solutions. The disruptive problems presented by alcoholic clients beg for effective responses rather than condemnation from the counselor. Yet guidelines for effective responses have often been lacking in approaches to alcoholism counseling.

The main purpose of this book is to fill that void: to provide practical intervention strategies for minimizing or eradicating those common problems that can doom the counseling experience to failure.

A second purpose is to describe and suggest remedies for certain problems that are more likely to be generated by the counselor than by clients.

Each disruptive problem is presented according to the following format: a) definition and description of the specific item (e.g. inconsistent attendance), b) discussion of variables that may have precipitated and/or maintained the problem (e.g. failure to confront the client candidly), and c) recommended strategies for managing the problem.

The strategies are pragmatic and straightforward. When theoretical material is necessary in order to explain complex behavior, the scientific definitions used are those that are most widely accepted.

Occasionally, a less than optimistic view is taken regarding the effectiveness of intervention. When the disruptive problem is highly resistant to change (e.g. denial), the factors that tend to retard progress are examined, the reasonable expectations of the counselor are discussed, and suggestions as to how the counselor might "work around" such behaviors are made.

Miller and Mastria (*Alternatives to Alcohol Abuse: A Social Learning Model*, 1977) are frequently cited as a resource for detailed explanations and valuable techniques pertaining to counseling alcoholic clients. Reading the entire book, which is available in paperback, is highly recommended.

Acknowledgments

I would like to express my gratitude to the many people whose assistance was invaluable to the publication of this book.

I am particularly grateful to Ms Blanche Horsham, head of the Addiction Research Foundation's Clinical Institute Out-patients' Department, and to her staff who helped define the problems.

I owe special appreciation to my editor, Ms Pat Ohlendorf, to Ms Barbara Rutledge, and to Mr. Donald Murray, whose assistance on the final drafts cannot be overly appreciated.

I am indebted to Mr. John LaRocque and Ms Marnie Marlie who provided me with the opportunity and time to pursue this project.

Finally, I am deeply grateful to my wife, Deborah, and to my friends, John Nkansah and Brian Green, whose continued support could always be counted on when I thought I'd never reach the point of actually writing these acknowledgments.

Introduction

During the past two decades there has been a proliferation of surveys concerned with attitudes of health and social service personnel towards alcoholics. Some general conclusions can be drawn. On the whole, members of the helping professions who work with alcoholics view the effects of their efforts with pessimism and frequently admit that they would prefer to work with clients whose prognoses are more favorable. Many look upon their helping role with what can best be described as a sense of resignation. Knox's research (1971) clearly indicates that the majority of those mental health workers with the most "prestigious" credentials would prefer to spend only a relatively small fraction of their work week in treating alcoholics and would strongly resist pressure to increase that amount of time significantly. Social workers acquitted themselves somewhat more favorably, but more than half of a large sample were unwilling to commit more than 25% of their work time to alcoholic clients (Knox, 1973).

This might be cause for despair if evidence showed a relationship between the type of credentials of the alcoholism counselor and the likelihood of a successful treatment outcome. But Armor et al. (1976), in one of the most ambitious studies of alcoholism treatment to date, found that the difference between successful outcome rates for clients treated with "therapy" by professionals (those holding "relevant" graduate school degrees) and clients receiving "counseling" by paraprofessionals (those not holding "relevant" graduate school degrees) was so slight as to be "hardly of any substantive significance."

Thus, although society has not expected paraprofessionals to play a primary role in treating alcoholic clients, their performance appears no less satisfactory than the performance of those with higher status degrees. Perhaps because paraprofessionals have elected to specialize in alcoholism counseling, they are less

1

likely to be resigned to their work than professionals, many of whom have been drafted. No doubt there are many with advanced degrees who have also chosen to specialize, but the ratio of paraprofessionals to professionals in alcoholism treatment is greater than 2:1 and is increasing (Alcohol and Drug Problems Association of North America, 1974).

For the sake of simplicity and because no difference in treatment success has been reported between the two groups, the distinction between "professional" and "paraprofessional" is not made in this book. All those who have counseling skills and are partly or wholly engaged in working with alcoholics are regarded as professionals, whether their degree is a two-year community college certificate or a doctor of medicine. Reference to specific professional groups is made only if their unique qualifications are required for specific treatment interventions (e.g. the prescription of medication, admitting privileges to a psychiatric facility, etc.).

Similarly, the terms "therapy" and "psychotherapy" (and the accompanying titles "therapist" and "psychotherapist") are avoided, and "counseling" is used instead. The distinction between therapy and counseling is unclear and often seems more related to status in a pecking order than to actual differences in the quality or nature of the interventions.

Developing treatment plans for any group of outpatients presents certain problems that cannot be controlled. This is particularly true in the case of alcoholics. Typically, an outpatient counselor spends one hour per week with each client. Even though that hour may be rewarding and reassuring for clients, there remain numerous provocations and reinforcements for drinking in the everyday environment; in a hospital setting, however, these influences are temporarily removed. In addition, while in an inpatient setting there are usually several staff members to design and institute a treatment plan, outpatient counselors must often rely only on themselves.

One might conclude, therefore, that for most alcoholics inpatient treatment is superior to outpatient treatment. This, however, has not been found to be the case (Baekeland et al., 1975).

Perhaps, instead, it is of greater benefit for clients to learn to contend with the provocative stimuli and potential reinforcements for drinking in their daily lives rather than being isolated in the artificial environment of a hospital. If one accepts this view, as do Lawrence (1961) and Miller and Mastria (1977), it then seems favorable to work with alcoholics on an outpatient basis wherever possible, despite the problems the outpatient counselor must face in managing clients' disruptive behaviors.

Strategies for dealing with the counterproductive behaviors of outpatient alcoholics are woefully underresearched, even though they are acknowledged to have a significantly negative effect on the treatment process. Therefore, as well as using the observations and commentary of writers who have worked extensively with alcoholics, the author must in several instances depend upon his own training and clinical experience in recommending treatment strategies.

Particularly frustrating for the alcoholism counselor is the fact that there *can be no* definitive strategy. Even though clients may manifest the same overt disruptive behavior, the same approach is not automatically called for, because each client is, ultimately, an individual. Murray and Jacobson (1971) correctly note that identical behavior by the counselor may facilitate responsiveness in some patients and inhibit it in others.

Differences between counselors must also be taken into account. Even counselors with similar treatment biases may differ markedly in their perception of the degree of disruptiveness of certain behaviors or characteristics to the treatment process. This was evident in the range of scores that resulted when the outpatient staff of the Addiction Research Foundation's Clinical Institute rated each of the disruptive problems addressed in this book. Counselors, like clients, are individuals.

Finally, disruptions cannot always be assumed to be the responsibility of clients. There are occasions when, wittingly or unwittingly, the counselor may induce or perpetuate in clients those very behaviors that impair the treatment process. This theme is expanded in later sections.

Before turning to the specific disruptive problems encountered in alcoholism treatment, some basic questions must be considered. What are the necessary conditions in order for treatment to take place? What are the initial goals?

Many authors seem to agree that what happens between counselor and clients is quite independent of the counselor's theoretical orientation. Lawrence (1961) states that the success of any treatment method depends upon the development of an effective counseling relationship. Lynn (1966) also proposes that this relationship probably takes precedence over any specific therapeutic modality. Forrest (1975) takes the issue one step further. While noting that a positive therapeutic relationship is mandatory for success, he continues, "I seriously doubt that psychotherapy has anything special to offer addicted individuals other than being a deeply meaningful human relationship" (p. 89). Forrest suggests that only through this human relationship, by means of emulation and modeling, can alcoholics change.

A slightly different, but relevant, point of view is taken by Mayer and Myerson (1971). After researching several treatment variables, they conclude that while the most significant variable is the counselor's ability to establish rapport with clients, the treatment-enhancing value of positive rapport may not be as significant as the detrimental effect of poor rapport. They found this to be the case regardless of the orientation of the counselor. A report of the Alcohol and Drug Problems Association of North America (1974) concerned with standards for evaluating the qualifications of workers in alcoholism treatment concludes that, above all, the "successful" counselor must have the ability to establish positive relationships with alcoholic clients.

If, as noted by Forrest (1975) and others, very few alcoholics actually want to stop drinking but for various reasons are compelled to seek treatment, the following observation of Milt

(1967) is understandable: the initial treatment encounter is likely to be with a hostile, obstructive, and uncooperative individual. Clearly, if this is the case, one cannot expect change to take place without patience, tolerance, and understanding on the part of the counselor. How can the initial goal of a positive relationship with alcoholic clients be achieved? For Moore (1972), the counselor must be a "nondoctrinaire" problem solver for whom "words" are less important than demonstrating "genuine concern" for clients. The counselor must be a willing and active intervenor, participant, and interpreter of reality. In Moore's "positive alliance" with alcoholic clients, passivity and ferreting out unconscious conflicts have no place. Edwards (1967), who apologizes for the lack of research evidence to support his assertions, agrees with Moore and adds that dependence is at times acceptable; the counselor should be directive when necessary, and orientation should be centred in the here and now. Both Chafetz (1959) and Gerard and Saenger (1966) recommend a similar approach, with particular attention to be paid to the feelings of low self-esteem so often encountered in alcoholic clients.

Despite the lack of empirical evidence among the cited authors, they are in considerable agreement, and their recommendations are very much in accord with Moberg's (1975) report on alcoholic clients' subjective evaluations of the "good therapist." (Behavioristically inclined treatment specialists would undoubtedly take exception to such unscientific terms as "positive alliance" and "meaningful human relationship," but the problem may be semantic. The hypothesis of Goldstein et al. — "Resistance in psychotherapy is reduced by training the patient to view the therapist as a positive but discriminating reinforcer" [1966:192] — fairly well approximates these less scientific terms.)

Although, as previously noted, this handbook is directed towards those with basic counseling skills, it is not necessarily assumed that all counselors are skilled in developing therapeutic relationships. Truax and Carkhuff (1967) have documented and examined three essential ingredients in positive treatment relationships: accurate understanding of clients, nonpossessive warmth, and genuineness, or authenticity. These have been demonstrated to be effective regardless of the counselor's theoretical orientation and are in consonance with the essentials described by alcoholism treatment specialists. If appropriate, the reader may choose to refer to Truax and Carkhuff as a useful resource for the enhancement of skills in this important area.

Frequently, the professional spends most of the first and possibly the second interview collecting information about clients, often at the expense of meaningful interaction. Noting that alcoholics commonly have a low tolerance for frustration, Chafetz (1959) recommends that the counselor be sensitive to this at the inception. Obviously, early and accurate history-taking is a responsibility of the professional, but concern for clients' apprehensions and anxieties is vital. What good is a comprehensive history if the client fails to return?

For the helping professional, an initial interview is a routine event. For alcoholics, both the anticipation and occurrence of the initial interview are likely to be quite stressful. Thus, the groundwork for a positive therapeutic relationship must begin at the beginning. Miller and Mastria (1977) recommend minimal data-gathering during the first interview. They suggest that the time be spent in identifying clients' immediate problems and concerns and in trying to provide positive outcome expectancy (i.e. the knowledge that alcoholics can recover). The method of assessing clients' problems during the first few sessions is described in detail by the authors (pp. 17-34).

Another significant part of the early stages of treatment is contracting. In order to help reduce future disruptive behavior, the responsibilities and goals of both clients and counselor should be clarified either orally or in writing. While the specifics of the contractual agreement may vary from client to client, it is necessary for all clients to acknowledge what is expected of them and to articulate their own goals. Clients must be active participants, not merely recipients of therapeutic wisdom and advice. This is *particularly* true for alcoholics. Depressive neurotics cannot contract to cease being depressed; neither can schizophrenics contract to stop hearing voices. These are passive experiences over which individuals have little control. The behaviors of alcoholics, however, are active and thus subject to control. Learning that it is possible to bring self-destructive patterns of behavior under control is, in the opinion of the author, critical to the process of recovery.

A contract should include not only an agreement of goals and responsibilities but also penalities for not living up to one's part of the bargain. Penalties must be things that are valued by clients. The author recalls an alcoholic who played bingo twice a week. During the initial phases of treatment the contract called for her attending AA not less than once a week. If she missed a meeting, she agreed to forfeit a bingo evening as well. Consumption of alcohol led to the stiffer penalty of forfeiting both bingo evenings.

Contracting helps prevent a situation in which counseling "drifts aimlessly" (Weiner, 1975), as there are clear objectives to serve as the nucleus of each session. Methods of goal setting, negotiating, and contracting are described in Miller and Mastria (pp. 40-48).

1

Denial

Forrest (1975) defines denial as the refusal to acknowledge the degree of control that alcohol has assumed in one's life. Any counselor experienced in working with alcoholics has heard over and over again, "I can quit if I want to," or "Sure I drink but I'm not an alcoholic." Deniers often refuse to accept the negative, even disastrous, effects of their drinking on themselves and their families and take refuge in the belief that others are overreacting. It is not uncommon for deniers to even attempt to enlist the support of the counselor in their belief that their drinking is not really as serious as others see it. Forrest remarks that denial is perhaps the most significant barrier to rehabilitation. Ewalt et al. (1957) go further, suggesting that treatment cannot proceed until clients are willing to accept that they are having difficulty controlling their drinking and that they need help. It is legitimate to ask why deniers are even willing to attend an initial appointment. Typically, external pressure from a spouse, boss, family doctor, etc. and a need to remain in the good graces of those applying pressure provide the initial motivation.

Variables to Consider
1. the need to deny
2. genuine deniers vs. public deniers
3. initial approaches in counseling
4. confrontation

Lambert (1971) offers three common reasons for denial:

1. because facing the reality of alcoholism can be very threatening, many alcoholics have rationalized their behavior for so long that they have developed "an almost reflex action" of defensiveness when challenged about their drinking;

2. the label of immorality so frequently linked in Western society

1. Denial

to alcoholism requires clients not only to accept their drinking problems but also to admit that they are "moral weakling[s] and/or . . . moral degenerate[s]"; and

3. the private and public acknowledgment of alcoholism requires alcoholics to accept that their lives must undergo radical change.

During the early phases of treatment it can be difficult to differentiate between clients who genuinely do not believe they have a problem and those who privately fear they can no longer control their drinking. One surefire way of losing clients before the distinction can be made is to demand total abstinence. Even if clients are willing to return, they are likely to be hostile and resistant, because the counselor has unwittingly compelled them to entrench their denial more deeply. Early confrontation with deniers is most ill-advised.

How then should the counselor proceed? The initial goal, which should be established in the first session, is to contract with clients to return. Accepting such clients' denial for the time being, the counselor should emphasize his or her willingness to begin treatment and point out to the clients that they have nothing to lose. If clients indicate that they have nothing to gain either, the counselor might say, "Perhaps we can sort out some of the pressures that are being exerted on you." The counselor is aware that deniers are likely to return due to the external pressures, but, by not prematurely tampering with their defenses, has probably made them feel more comfortable. Furthermore, contracting with clients to return allows them to make a personal commitment, which will likely reduce the anger they might feel at having been coerced into treatment.

It is appropriate to discuss alcohol use during the early counseling sessions as long as it is done in an *unthreatening* manner. Topics might include: "Are there ever times when it is difficult for you to handle alcohol?" "Have you ever thought of cutting down?" "How do you think your life might change if you cut down or quit?" "Let's examine why your spouse is so upset about your drinking." In this warming-up period the counselor's goal should be to establish a therapeutic relationship, and Milt's recommended qualities of patience, tolerance, and understanding should prevail.

Only after deniers feel comfortable in the relationship should the counselor risk confrontation (Glasser, 1965) — and as Truax and Mitchell (1971) report, confrontation is a valid part of the treatment process. The counselor should confront such clients in a candid, low-key manner, attempting to elicit what Ewalt et al. suggest is the prerequisite for treatment: recognition of the drinking problem and the need for help. At this point, when a trusting relationship has been established, the differentiation between genuine and public deniers can often easily be made. Confrontation may not even be necessary with public deniers, who may voluntarily take the risk of admitting to a drinking problem. Public deniers are often relieved by their own admission and overly apologetic for having withheld.

What should the counselor say when confronting clients? Timing is important, and often the behavior of clients will dictate when confrontation is most appropriate. A marital crisis related to alcohol abuse or even a hangover may serve as a lead in to confrontation. Employing a supportive and nonjudgmental approach, the counselor might say, "I guess we're going to have to take a closer look at your drinking," "It seems like things are getting out of hand," or "Maybe it's time we discuss how you can cut down." Public deniers are likely to be responsive. Genuine deniers, on the other hand, whose defenses are strong, all too frequently find ways of rationalizing, regardless of what has happened. Even a mild confrontation may evoke an angry response or may be used as justification for dropping out of treatment. If genuine deniers do not terminate at this point and can "work through" their anger, the counselor is that much the wiser about the defensiveness of such clients and the probability of overreaction in future confrontations.

Research by O'Leary et al. (1977) suggests that denial may be an adaptive component of the recovery process for some alcoholics — a part of the individual's style of coping with stress. They recommend that treatment efforts move away from confrontation towards the development of behavioral skills to reduce anxiety. It is questionable, however, whether this advice is applicable to the outpatient setting. The 54 patients in the study were hospitalized; about half of them dropped out of outpatient follow-up within a year, and another 19 were rehospitalized. Thus, the study's data and recommendations can at best be viewed as suggestive.

It would appear, then, that the continued treatment of genuine deniers (assuming their willingness to continue) may well depend upon the counselor's tolerance for frustration, other time commitments, and the quality of the counseling relationship thus far. But things cannot, as Weiner (1975) puts it, "drift aimlessly." Even at the risk of losing clients, the counselor must now make greater demands, such as including spouses in the sessions, asking clients, in spite of continued denying, to reassess their drinking with an eye towards reducing alcohol consumption, or even suspending treatment temporarily in order for clients to reconsider their drinking behavior. Realistically, chances are high that deniers will terminate at this point. The counselor can take solace in knowing that he or she has done all that can be reasonably expected.

Some final notes concerning deniers: Insight-oriented counseling (i.e. that concerned with the causes of drinking) has been shown to be unsuccessful in the treatment of alcoholics (Boylin, 1975). Given their deeply embedded defenses, this technique would be particularly fruitless in the case of genuine deniers. Placing genuine deniers in a group of alcoholics may have an impact, however. Peer group discussion and the chance to compare their own drinking behavior with that of other group members may encourage deniers to reassess themselves.

2

Continued Drinking while in Treatment

Chafetz (1967) views the continued use of alcohol while in treatment in the following manner:

> *The therapist must deal with alcohol as a psychological defense: the pharmacological effect of alcohol allows the formation of an emotional and intellectual barrier between patient and therapist, and therapeutic efforts are blunted. The lack of this barrier should not be held out as a precondition for therapy, but its removal should be an early goal for effective progress. (p. 1025)*

These remarks fairly well summarize the comments made by other writers who have addressed this subject. Chafetz continues with an additional significant point:

> *Therapists dealing with alcohol problems cannot use rigid approaches but must be daring and inventive with each patient and circumstance. (p. 1026)*

Thus, Chafetz suggests that it is unrealistic both to prolong clients' drinking behavior indefinitely and to demand immediate termination of alcohol use. A reasonable position to take is that clients must *try* to remain abstinent during treatment (Ewalt, et al., 1957). To be "inventive" with each client and circumstances is to recognize that what may work with one individual may have no effect or even a negative effect on another. Thus, Miller and Mastria (1977), while proposing an overall framework for a treatment plan, emphasize the importance of assessing the unique needs of each client and adapting the framework to the individual.

Variables to Consider
1. abstinence early in treatment
2. drinking as a lifestyle
3. contracting
4. confrontation
5. self-control and alternatives

13

2. Continued Drinking

It is a naive counselor who insists upon immediate abstinence rather than viewing it as an early goal. True, some clients may submit, but more often this approach leads to dishonesty and the feeling on the clients' part of "putting one over" on the counselor. Many alcoholics with whom the author has worked have described the ends to which they will go in order to hide or play down their drinking. Necessity has turned many alcoholics into experts at deception. It is not uncommon for an unsophisticated counselor to be lulled into believing that real progress is being made, only to find out later (perhaps by a call from a spouse) that clients have been drinking regularly. The counselor may then feel angry, frustrated, and even inclined to terminate treatment. If the counselor stresses that it is important for clients to be honest about their drinking behavior and simultaneously assures confidentiality and a nondisciplinary attitude, he or she is less likely to be deceived. Only when clients feel secure enough to be honest can the counselor learn about their drinking behavior and the conditions under which it occurs.

It must be kept in mind that drinking is not an isolated behavior but a lifestyle. Consider alcoholics who congregate with their "drinking buddies" after work, who never watch television without a supply of beer on hand, who feel worthwhile only when drinking, who use alcohol to blunt unhappiness with job, marriage, and financial insecurity, and who, through alcohol, can release harbored resentments and other repressed feelings. Insistence on immediate abstinence without taking into account the numerous alcohol-related aspects of clients' lives could lead to speedy drop-out. Counselor and clients must discuss the inevitable: that giving up alcohol will require other changes as well.

These remarks by no means preclude suggesting, in the initial interview, that clients give abstinence a try before any specific treatment plans are instituted. At the same time, clients should be advised to keep a record of any alcohol consumption: when and where it occurred, how much was consumed, and how they felt prior to consumption. This information will be valuable in future planning.

If clients continue to drink during the first few sessions —

14

the period of assessment and laying the groundwork for a therapeutic relationship — then a contract must be drawn up calling for a sincere effort to abstain completely. Also, for the time being, clients should avoid situations that typically evoke drinking and should keep no alcohol at home.

Clients should recommend their own penalties for breaking the contract, and penalties must be things of personal value: donating money to charity, not watching a favorite television program, not engaging in a pleasurable activity, doing an unpleasant chore, etc. (Clients generally suggest much harsher penalties than would the counselor.) Making sure that clients recommend the disciplinary action avoids forcing the counselor to act in a punitive and authoritarian manner. It is the clients — not the counselor — who take responsibility and pay the price for their behavior.

During the difficult transitional period the counselor must be as supportive as possible, giving praise and encouragement, and taking a nonjudgmental attitude towards "slips." This is a critical period, because, as Chafetz notes, progress is unlikely to occur without abstinence. It is at this time that the inventiveness of the counselor comes into play, for he or she must take an active role in helping clients find new and interesting activities not related to alcohol, and new ways of coping with stress (e.g. relaxation training, which is described in detail by Miller and Mastria, pp. 49-62).

A tactical problem may occur if clients continue with alcohol consumption on a fairly regular basis. All too often, counselors attempt to play this behavior down, hoping that with further counseling the problem will take care of itself. It won't! Candid and constructive confrontation is necessary. It must be acknowledged that progress is not taking place, and the reasons must be explored.

The fault does not always lie with clients. In some instances the continued drinking may be due to something the counselor has overlooked or underestimated. Perhaps, for example, the counselor was not sufficiently inventive in suggesting alternative activities to drinking.

2. Continued Drinking

If the counselor genuinely believes that he or she is not at fault, then in a nonaccusatory manner clients should be told that it is time to decide on the most appropriate course of action. If clients complain that hostility at home is responsible for their continued drinking, then conjoint therapy should be undertaken. If they believe job pressure is responsible, then alternative employment should be considered. Whatever the issues, clients must agree to try to come to terms with them. This means that in order for treatment to continue, the contract must be renegotiated. This should not be presented as a threat but as a necessary step if the drinking behavior is to be brought under control. The counselor should make sure that clients understand that this action is being taken because the counselor cares.

If drinking continues after attempts have been made to resolve the relevant issues, the next step is a repeat: confrontation again. By this time, such clients must be prepared to face their inability to manage their alcohol intake. The author recommends that disulfiram (Antabuse*) be taken on a daily basis.

Many alcoholic clients resist this recommendation because they view the drug as a "crutch." Their cooperation may depend on the manner in which the drug is recommended to them. While Antabuse *is* a crutch, it is also an "insurance policy." When taking Antabuse, clients are compelled to think twice about having a drink because of the very unpleasant consequences they will experience even if small amounts of alcohol are consumed (e.g. nausea, possibly severe headache, chest pain). In a sense, they are buying time for the urge to pass; they can deal constructively with the urge by attempting to relax or by contacting the counselor for support and reassurance. Antabuse should be viewed as a temporary measure while the counselor continues to work with clients on adjustment problems, giving particular attention to the conditions under which the urge to drink has occurred. (Further discussion of Antabuse as compared with less desirable alternatives is found in Section 16: "Refusal to Take Medication.")

*Registered trademark of Ayerst Laboratories.

In addition to taking Antabuse, those clients who are having great difficulty in abstaining should be "saturated" with as many leisure-time activities as possible. It must not be forgotten that those many hours previously devoted exclusively to drinking are, if not adequately filled, likely to continue to impede progress.

For example, attending AA meetings need not be a once-a-week venture. In larger communities it is possible to attend a meeting virtually every night of the week, or even more than once a day for the highly motivated. Hospitals, community services, and other nonprofit organizations welcome volunteers. Night school and other skill development programs may also be considered. Social activities sponsored by church and community organizations should be encouraged.

3

Relapse

Relapse is different from continued drinking while in treatment in that a significant period (at least three to four weeks) of abstinence is maintained prior to a return to alcohol abuse. There is little relevant literature on the subject with the exception of Marlatt's finding that "social pressure from friends is one of the major precipitants of relapse in alcoholics" (Miller and Mastria, 1977:8). Although it is common knowledge, supported by Gerard and Saenger (1966), that the majority of alcoholic clients tend to relapse after treatment is completed, we are here concerned only with the problem of relapse while in treatment.

Variables to Consider
1. lapse
2. strategies for preventing relapse
3. binge drinking
4. counselor-related relapse
5. direction of treatment after relapse

The counselor's response to resumed alcohol use should correspond to the severity of the relapse. A "lapse," or brief return to alcohol, is often due to experimenting with controlled intake. The results are predictable: clients drink considerably more than they intended. It is often best to respond to a lapse in a low-key, sympathetic, and brief manner — *definitely not* with an "I told you so" approach. Indeed, a lapse may be viewed as a good object lesson: experimenting can be dangerous. Furthermore, such clients probably will have incurred the wrath of their spouses, will feel guilty about their behavior, and embarrassed about discussing the incident. The counselor should give clients the benefit of the doubt and treat the experience as productive.

But a relapse, or major resumption of alcohol abuse, has far

19

3. Relapse

more serious implications. The author has found that in clients with previously good attendance records, relapse is often the reason for missing an appointment or even dropping out of treatment completely.

As noted in Section 2 ("Continued Drinking while in Treatment"), it is helpful for the counselor to know when and where drinking usually takes place, and how clients feel prior to consumption. Until counselor and client agree that there has been sufficient improvement, the counselor should be adamant on this point: clients must avoid situations which in the past have elicited drinking behavior. A client with a history of relapses may have to avoid such situations indefinitely. Unfortunately, however, in some instances avoidance is not possible. When drinking is associated with the home, for example, alternative home activities and specific relaxation exercises are necessary, as well as a *firm* commitment to have no alcoholic beverages in the house.

Most important, the counselor must attempt to deal with the feelings of stress that have evoked drinking in the past. These antecedent feelings can often be altered through general relaxation training (see Miller and Mastria) and/or deconditioning clients' responses to specific situations of stress (e.g. social events).

If clients do not respond well to relaxation training, the *temporary* and closely supervised use of tranquillizers may be helpful as an adjunct. Although most physicians are understandably cautious about prescribing tranquillizers for chronic alcoholics, the author has found them to be quite cooperative when informed — *with clients' consent* — that the clients are undergoing alcoholism treatment. Tranquillizers may occasionally be prescribed for longer than a few weeks *only* when relaxation training techniques have clearly failed and when the counselor is confident that such clients have been continuously abstinent. However, because of the distinct possibility of abuse of and dependence on tranquillizers in previously alcohol-dependent people, a definite time period (two to three months at most) should be agreed upon. Ultimately, clients must learn to cope with stress without resorting to alcohol or pills. And that must be a key long-range goal of counseling.

Even with the counselor's support and the successful mastery of relaxation, or tranquillizer-induced relaxation, unanticipated events may provoke a relapse. Clients do not live in a vacuum; it is not possible to anticipate all of the external contingencies that may cause severe stress reactions.

Nevertheless, a relapse may be avoided by helping clients learn how to deal with the unexpected. One useful means is role playing, where, in the carefully controlled conditions of the counselor's office, client and counselor act out examples of unanticipated stressful situations (e.g. criticism by the boss or a major argument over a minor incident at home). In each instance, the counselor should make a real effort to produce stress. Then client and counselor develop a strategy for coping with each stressful situation in ways other than drinking. For example, after "criticism by the boss," a client might imagine leaving the office temporarily (possibly to a lounging area or to her car) and employing the relaxation techniques she has learned. Or, similarly, following a "marital argument," another client might imagine removing himself to another room and using relaxation exercises. In each situation the counselor remains passive until the client reports feeling relaxed. The greater the variety of role-playing situations that are acted out to successful resolutions, the greater the probability of generalizing to new situations.

Another technique is training clients to act out in their imaginations angry or even violent responses to those people who elicit stress. This method is particularly useful with passive clients. The imaginary acting out of suppressed anger can be a gratifying, tension-relieving experience. In order for either role playing or imaginary acting out to be effective, they must be practised regularly. The latter technique, obviously, can be practised more easily at home.

To help clients become more assertive in appropriate situations, a more action-oriented approach may be taken. In alcoholics, frequent antecedents to drinking are the feelings of frustration and anger towards themselves caused by behaving nonassertively when assertiveness is called for. Assertiveness can be learned along with role playing and imaginary acting out, both of which are more concerned with instances where direct assertion may not be appropriate. (Assertiveness training is described in detail by Miller and Mastria, 1977:63-81.)

One form of relapse requires a more specialized approach: "binge" drinking. Typically, binge drinkers go for weeks or even months without consuming alcohol. Then, for what appears to be no reason, they drink an extraordinary amount, usually over a period of several days. The counselor often observes a speedy return to total abstinence in such clients. They are usually discharged with considerable optimism, only to return a few months later after another binge.

After careful observation of and discussion with such clients, the author has recognized a pattern that occurs during the few days prior to the binge. The individual becomes irritable and anxious, grows increasingly hostile and argumentative at the slightest provocation, becomes preoccupied with alcohol, and behaves erratically. Due to the extreme disruptiveness of the binge, family members usually do not connect it to the preexistent behavior. Therefore, in counseling such a client, the family should be included. They must be taught to read the signs of an upcoming binge and to respond effectively. The client's counselor should be contacted, and he or she should make the effort to see client and family as soon as possible. The alcoholic's physician should also be alerted because often brief hospitalization, sedation, or both may be advisable.

But what is the counselor to do when, despite good rapport and the seeming success of preventive strategies, relapse occurs? Because, as noted earlier, missed appointments or drop-out are common after relapse, the first thing the counselor should do is to send such clients a letter specifying another appointment. If they do return, they are likely to be fearful of rejection, so reassurance and understanding on the part of the counselor are necessary.

As with other disruptive behaviors, the counselor must consider the possibility of his or her own contribution to the relapse. Both Selzer (1957) and Chafetz (1967) have remarked that negative or rejecting feelings expressed by the counselor might lead to continued drinking or relapse. Even though clients are abstaining and attending counseling sessions regularly, they may be feeling no better or may, however incorrectly, believe that the counselor doesn't really care. Relapse can also occur if treatment is drifting aimlessly. Granted, it may not be possible for the counselor to sufficiently demonstrate to some clients that he or she does care. Clients with histories of rejection may be unwilling to accept that anyone could care about them. But if the counselor is aware of any hostility towards certain clients or feels that treatment is indeed drifting aimlessly, corrective measures must be taken. There should be no shame in a counselor acknowledging that he or she may not be the best person to be working with a particular client. Referral to someone else may be in the client's best interest.

In most instances, however, the counselor does not contribute significantly to relapse. Regardless of what is happening in treatment, relapse may occur because of lack of support outside the counselor's office or inappropriate support from drinking friends. When it happens, the counselor should act as a reality-oriented problem solver, quickly attempting to pinpoint why the relapse occurred and assessing the damage it may have caused. It is helpful if the counselor can assure such clients that he or she has worked with other clients who have relapsed and have gone on to improve afterwards.

Increasing the number of sessions per week after relapse is usually a mistake, because it can lead to increased dependence on the counselor. AA should be seriously considered, as it provides the continuing additional support of others who have had similar experiences and are now succeeding. Counseling should continue in a nonjudgmental atmosphere, with the counselor giving more direct attention to helping clients improve their stress-coping skills. The agreement to avoid settings that have elicited drinking behavior should also be reaffirmed.

Because many alcoholics tend to be overly punitive towards themselves after relapse, the counselor's approach should be, "We can't change what has happened; we must work harder to keep it from happening again."

4
Motivation

"Probably in no other illness is so much verbal concern manifested for the patient's motivation to recover as in alcoholism" (Pittman and Sterne, 1965:41). Moore and Buchanan (1964), in a nationwide survey of U.S. state hospitals, and Moore (1971), in a similar study of U.S. private hospitals, both found that more than 70% of reporting hospitals attributed their relatively unsuccessful results in the treatment of alcoholics to poor motivation.

Looking at the problem from another perspective, it is clear that alcoholics are usually quite motivated *to continue drinking* (Forrest, 1975). Thus, Fox (1958) comments that no alcoholic will consider abstaining until alcohol brings more "suffering" than "pleasure;" alcohol abuse must cause the loss of something important or at least seriously threaten such a loss. In support of this view, Lemere et al. (1958) report that few, if any, alcoholics stop drinking unless they are seriously pressured, and Gerard et al. (1962), who followed up 400 discharged alcoholic clients, conclude that the most influential factor in continued abstinence is fear. Personal crises, according to Trice (1966), usually cause alcoholics to abstain only temporarily.

It is hardly surprising, therefore, that 89% of the psychiatrists surveyed by Glasscote et al. (1967) considered alcoholics to be "more difficult" or "much more difficult" to treat than other clients. Another 2% described them as "impossible" to treat.

Variables to Consider
1. competing motivational states
2. latent positive motivations
3. common errors by the counselor
4. coercion

25

4. Motivation

The literature strongly suggests that what motivates alcoholics to seek help from a counselor and possibly to continue in treatment is the desire to avoid serious negative consequences. One inference is that alcoholics do not seek assistance as much to gain something as not to lose something. A second inference is that the motivating fear must be maintained in order for abstinence to continue.

Although avoidance motivation may apply to many alcoholics in counseling, the following examples suggest that it is not all-encompassing:

1. An alcoholic is coerced into treatment by legal authorities. In order to avoid unpleasant consequences, she attends her sessions but continues to drink because her primary motivation is continued alcohol consumption. Coercion does not lead to a change in behavior for this client, as there is no penalty for continued drinking.

2. An alcoholic attempts to abstain because his wife is threatening to leave him. He experiences competing motivational states, wanting to continue drinking but at the same time wanting to abstain at least temporarily. As any student of basic psychology is aware, prior behaviors resume when the negative reinforcement is removed or reduced to a tolerable level. Thus, once this alcoholic learns that his wife is not carrying out her threat to leave, he is likely to resume drinking. (Motivation to drink remains, while the competing motivation to abstain is no longer present.)

3. Another alcoholic finds that when she drinks at night she is unable to perform even routine tasks. She would like to advance in her profession, but this requires homework. She seeks help in order to improve the situation. (Motivation to drink remains but is in direct competition with a *positive* motivation.)

4. In still another situation, an alcoholic learns that he has advanced cirrhosis. His alcoholism has compelled him to avoid social functions, to have little sexual contact with his wife, and to be unable to enjoy activities with his children. This client is motivated both to continue drinking and, due to his medical

condition, to abstain. In addition, however, there may be a latent motivation to enhance the quality of his life: he has something to gain through abstinence even though he may not be consciously aware of it. By dealing with the here and now, the counselor can help this client appreciate the positive aspects of abstinence.

In none of the above examples are clients "unmotivated." What is at issue is the direction and strength of the motivation. It is worth noting that in the previously cited survey (Glasscote et al., 1967), 9% of the psychiatrists questioned *did not* find alcoholics more difficult to treat than other clients. Curlee (1971) suggests that the larger percentage of psychiatrists were probably dealing with the pathology without giving much attention to the symptom: the drinking itself. Probably true! But what about the 9% who had as much success with alcoholics as they did with other clients? Could it be that by directing their attention towards the symptom, they were concerned not only with the adverse consequences of continued drinking, but also with the advantages to be gained through abstinence?

There is evidence that many alcoholics do improve (Bahn et al., 1963; Emrick, 1975; Trice, 1966; Baekeland et al., 1975). At the same time, there appears to be no evidence that improvement relates to any particular form of treatment (Armor et al., 1976). The author suggests, on the basis of his own experience, that those alcoholics who improve do so not only out of fear but also out of latent positive motives and the ability of the counselor to capitalize on these potentials. All too often, alcoholism counselors are prophets of doom — "If you don't practise what I preach, there will be dire consequences." Although fear is without question a powerful motivator, its value is limited to the continued presence of the fear-motivating circumstances. The counselor must seek, *with clients,* positive reinforcements for continued abstinence.

This point is most accurately expressed by Miller and Mastria:

> *The counselor must evaluate the client's difficulty in self-managing in terms of what she, the counselor, is doing (or not doing) rather than in terms of motivation of the client.*

> *The counselor should not be saying, 'What is wrong with
> the client? Why isn't she taking my advice?' The counselor
> should be asking, 'What must I do to increase the likelihood
> that the client will engage in self-management behaviors?'*
> *(1977:141)*

Another common error leads the counselor to believe that clients are inappropriately motivated. Larkin (1974), Strupp (1971), and Moore (1964) note that the counselor's communications are often at odds with clients' expectations. The counselor may attempt to deal almost exclusively with the unconscious conflicts or psychosocial problems underlying the drinking behavior, while clients expect to be treated for their alcoholism. When the understandably frustrated clients terminate treatment, they are viewed by the counselor as inappropriately motivated. Weiner's opinion (1975) in this matter cannot be too strongly emphasized. He concludes that there is *no* empirical evidence to indicate that behavior change requires self-understanding or cannot occur without it.

A further word about fear is in order. Scare tactics can backfire and cause clients to withdraw from treatment. As Goldstein et al. (1966) report, "Resistance to psychotherapy is reduced as the threat value of the therapeutic communications is decreased" (p. 168). Conversely, no matter how valid the counselor's comments may be, increasing their "threat value" creates greater resistance, probable drop-out, and often the false conclusion that clients are inappropriately motivated. Thus, the client with cirrhosis should not be reminded again and again that alcohol is killing him. He knows!

The term "coercion" means that clients were unwilling to seek treatment on their own, regardless of whether they believe they have a problem. Should a counselor accept clients who have been coerced into treatment? Some prominent authors say "no" on both moral grounds (Strupp, 1971) and therapeutic grounds (Wolberg, 1967). The problem for the alcoholism counselor is that a large proportion of prospective clients *have* been coerced. It is a dilemma with no ready solution.

There are three major sources of coercion: family, employer, and the courts. Family coercion, typically from spouses, may under certain circumstances provide clients with sufficient reason to abstain and seek treatment. This is particularly true if spouses "push" rather than "threaten," if they are willing to be active participants in the alcoholics' treatment, if they understand and accept how painful abstinence may be, if they provide support and positive reinforcement (i.e. praise and affection) for abstinence, and, possibly most important, if they try to overcome their justifiable anger at their partners' past behavior. This is a lot to ask of any person. But husbands and wives of alcoholics who want their spouses to abstain and are committed to their marriages must meet the clients halfway. Under these conditions conjoint counseling, in addition to individual treatment for the alcoholics, is advised.

Employer coercion or, as Trice (1966) puts it, "constructive" coercion, is often effective due to the real threat of losing one's means of support. Unlike threatening spouses who may back down, employers are fully prepared to terminate employment. In "constructive" coercion, alcoholics are confronted with irrefutable evidence of their impairment, such as poor work attendance, poor work performance, or drinking on the job. Such clients are likely to be appropriately motivated, albeit by fear.

Legal coercion, or court-mandated treatment, is a different matter. Typically, such individuals are poor risks for treatment. They are required to be sober for their counseling sessions, but more often than not that is their *only* obligation. If treatment is undertaken, it should be carried out in close collaboration with parole or probation officers, and strict controls must be agreed upon from the outset, such as the use of Antabuse. (A possible exception to strict controls is described in Section 21: *"Social Class and Culture."*)

5

Inconsistent Attendance

Among the outpatient staff of the Addiction Research Foundation's Clinical Institute, inconsistent attendance is considered to be *the most* disruptive influence on the counseling process. One research study addresses this issue, and its results are important. Panepinto and Higgins (1969) arranged, after missed appointments, for clients to be sent letters the next day offering a new appointment for the following week. Similar letters were sent after two consecutive missed appointments. The result was a significant reduction in missed appointments. Such a simple, straightforward, and effective procedure should not be dismissed.

Variables to Consider
1. initial contract specifying regular attendance
2. counselor responsibility in the "caring" relationship
3. following through with continued missed appointments
4. misuse of attendance

One part of the initial contract should be an explicit understanding that clients attend their counseling sessions regularly. It is necessary but not sufficient for the counselor to say, "I expect you to attend your appointments." Clients must be told the reasons for the agreement: a) "I want to help you, and in order to do that I must see you on a regular basis," b) "Your coming regularly demonstrates to me that you want that help," and c) "I set aside the time for *you*." Implicit in the agreement is the counselor's message, "I am interested in what happens to you." As Panepinto and Higgins (1969) note, clients who habitually anticipate rejection receive instead genuine concern for their well-being. These authors view the interaction in the following manner: "The more the therapist is seen as wanting to help the

31

5. Inconsistent Attendance

patient, the more the patient will be motivated to continue the relationship and be influenced by the therapist." (p. 419)

The suggestion of Panepinto and Higgins to write a letter after a missed appointment appears in most instances to be preferable to a telephone call. A letter is neutral and nonjudgmental, and although it conveys only a simple message, it also serves to remind clients of the counselor's genuine concern. A telephone call, no matter how well intentioned, will likely put clients on the defensive, making them feel an explanation is necessary even when none has been asked for.

How should the counselor contend with clients who continue to miss appointments? Inconsistent attendance is both a drain on the counselor's time and a fairly clear indication of inappropriate motivation at that time. The counselor must confront clients with their consistent "breach of contract" and offer them the opportunity to either suspend treatment or "live up to their part of the bargain." This choice need not be presented as a threat. The counselor might say, "We seem to be accomplishing very little. Do you really think it's best to continue?" If clients choose to do so, it must be understood that further missed appointments will mean suspension of treatment. The term "suspension" (as opposed to "termination") is important. It implies that the counselor still cares and that the door remains open if clients decide to commit themselves to regular attendance.

A variation on the same theme is clients appearing for counseling sessions only during crises or personal difficulties. This must not be tolerated! Continuously permitting this behavior merely reinforces such clients' inappropriate use of the counseling situation; in effect the counselor is saying to them, "My role is to rescue you, not to help you manage your own problems" (Steiner, 1969). Crisis intervention may be part of the treatment of some clients who attend regularly (indeed, it may serve to strengthen their belief in the counselor's genuine concern) but it is not a substitute for regular treatment. The author has handled such clients by giving them the telephone number of a local crisis centre and saying clearly, "I will see you *only* if you are willing to come every week." It might be argued that this action constitutes rejection. Not true! Clients have been given the terms under which they *will be accepted.* Responsible behavior should be reinforced; irresponsible behavior should not.

6

Mistrust

Despite the essential value of trust in a treating relationship (Forrest, 1975), there is very little literature on the subject. Perhaps because trust seems so obvious, treatment experts have assumed that every counselor recognizes its significance. But there appear to be some sound reasons why trust should not be taken for granted, particularly in the treatment of alcoholics.

Variables to Consider
1. sources of mistrust
2. earning trust
3. testing

Because many alcoholic clients have had previous treatment experiences that have ended in failure, they may ask themselves, "Is there any cause for placing my trust in *this* counselor?" In addition, these clients may become bewildered, frustrated, and distrustful when their expectations of practical treatment seem opposed to the counselor's concern with probing the underlying dynamics of their drinking. Such clients may wonder, "How can I trust someone who won't address the reason I came here?" Closely related to this is Weiner's assessment (1975) of incorrect interpretations of clients' behavior, which often lead clients to question the counselor's capacity to understand them: "I believe I drink because alcohol increases my confidence when I'm with people, but the counselor says my drinking is due to an unresolved Oedipal conflict. How can I trust this person to be effective in treating me?"

Similar doubts may arise in clients when the counselor presents ill-timed or premature interpretations. (The author has known counselors who attempt to interpret client behavior as early as the initial interview.) The counselor who expresses over-confidence in his or her ability to help only lays the groundwork for mistrust when treatment fails to live up to the unrealistic expectations. (This is different from reassuring clients that alcoholics can be helped with a lot of hard work from both clients and counselor.) Another source of mistrust is the erratic counselor, who sometimes appears genuinely concerned and involved, and at other times seems indifferent. Clients usually see through the inadequately trained counselor or one who doubts his or her abilities, and soon decide that they cannot trust the counselor's recommendations. Finally, a reality of working with certain alcoholic clients who are socially isolated or deeply disturbed is that they are often unable to trust anyone.

The development of a trusting relationship depends to a large extent upon the counselor's appreciation that trust does not come about automatically. Indeed, clients who put too much faith and trust in the counselor prematurely may suffer considerable disappointment in the long run. In the first or second interview the counselor must introduce the subject of trust in a realistic manner, making it clear to clients that trust on both sides must be earned. In order to earn the trust of clients, the counselor must come across as a "real person" rather than as "playing God," must be realistic and candid about treatment rather than depending on a "mystique," must be consistent, genuinely concerned, appreciate clients' problems in the here and now, and assure them of confidentiality.

Because feelings of low self-esteem frequently lead alcoholics to expect rejection, they often "test" to reassure themselves that the counselor can indeed be trusted. It is not uncommon for clients to break a specific contractual agreement just to see how the counselor will react (Milt, 1967). If the counselor is prepared for the possibility of being tested, such an occurrence should not present a major problem. Even when the counselor believes that a certain action (e.g. calling late at night or canceling an appointment at the last moment) is probably a test, it is unnecessary to respond with a discussion about trust; neither is it cause for the counselor to stand trial. Typically, early testing behavior ceases when clients learn that the counselor responds matter-of-factly, without explanations in his or her defense. In addition — and to the dismay of the counselor — bending over backwards in a "you can trust me" posture often merely encourages such clients to set up new situations to find out just how far the counselor can be trusted.

7

Counselor's Hostility towards Clients

Catanzaro (1968) suggests that there may be reasons other than poor prognosis to account for the reluctance of many counselors to treat alcoholic clients. Negative feelings often stem from the belief that alcoholics so often violate social norms: aggressiveness when drinking, excessive dependency when sober, and frequent lack of cooperation in treatment. Supporting this belief is Mayfield's finding (1976) that the vast majority of those convicted of violent crimes have a history of problem drinking, and most were in fact under the influence of alcohol when they committed the violent act.

The question then arises whether a positive attitude towards clients is necessary for counselors to be effective. According to Rogers (1957), Wolberg (1967), and Strupp (1971), among many others, the answer is yes: a positive attitude towards clients is the overriding key to therapeutic influence, regardless of the counselor's treatment orientation. Moore (1965) strongly recommends that those counselors who feel uncomfortable working with alcoholics should not treat them. He notes that this is in the best interests of both client and counselor, for treatment is unlikely to be productive.

Variables to Consider
1. the initial interview
2. possible results of the counselor's hostility
3. genuine anger at clients' behavior

Moore's recommendation clearly implies that counselors with strong negative feelings towards alcoholics should not even agree to an initial interview; it would be more appropriate to refer the prospective clients to a less biased counselor. The author has observed that most counselors hold an ambivalent attitude towards alcoholics, their positive or negative feelings depending, to a large extent, on the individual alcoholic. For such counselors, an initial interview is appropriate. If the counselor then experiences negative or hostile feelings for whatever reason, treatment should not be undertaken. All too often, treatment that begins with the counselor attempting to work through negative feelings leads to unnecessary and damaging consequences for clients. A *degree* of tact is advisable, rather than stating reasons for outright rejection. The counselor might say, "I don't believe I'm the best person to be working with you. I'll try to find a more appropriate counselor as soon as possible." The client may walk away feeling somewhat rejected, disappointed, confused, and possibly angry. As guilt-arousing as that may be for the counselor, the long-range considerations should take precedence. If possible, alternative arrangements should be made prior to the client's leaving. In any event, it is the counselor's responsibility to act quickly and to then contact the client regarding the alternative arrangements.

More often, however, the counselor continues with treatment out of the self-deceiving view that one should not feel hostility or anger towards clients. According to Moore (1972), the guilt the counselor feels over his or her hostile feelings may lead to excessive permissiveness. For Moore, this is the "hallmark of endless therapeutic do-nothing-ness," until the client "either drifts away or is given enough rope to hang himself." Another possibility is described by Selzer (1957). Unwilling to either accept the hostility or make alternative arrangements, the counselor (presumably unwittingly) resorts to "therapeutic attacks" such as impatience, ill-timed direct interpretation, overcontrol, and outright rejection. In Selzer's opinion, such conditions can perpetuate drinking or lead to relapse. Chafetz (1967) observes that although the counselor may not be aware of it, clients easily pick up hostility, a situation that cannot help but be counterproductive. Steiner (1969) goes so far as to describe such a counselor as a "persecutor" whose increasing impatience can lead to increasingly hostile behavior on his or her part.

It seems conclusive, therefore, that if a counselor dislikes a client there can be no valid reason for continuing treatment. A transfer to another counselor is called for.

It is important to differentiate between the negative or hostile feelings that have just been described and the anger that results from inappropriate or disruptive behavior by clients — a common situation in treatment. A counselor may have very positive feelings about clients and yet feel genuine annoyance at their behavior. In many instances it is reasonable, even desirable, to express such angry feelings; it is possible, in fact, that attempting to suppress them may lead to more general negative feelings and hostility.

Anger need not suggest punitiveness or rejection. Developing the positive therapeutic relationship so strongly stressed by alcoholism treatment specialists requires honesty not only on the part of the client but of the counselor as well. The expression of anger should be viewed as a responsibility of the counselor and as a "barometer" for clients to read. Part of the contract between client and counselor should be, "If you behave inappropriately, I will respond with accurate feeling." To Moore (1972), the honest expression of feelings is an integral part of the counselor's role as active intervenor, participant, and interpreter of reality. Furthermore, it aids in establishing controls for clients, which Chafetz (1959) views to be essential in treating alcoholics.

8

Clients' Hostility towards the Counselor

Contrary to popular belief, most sober alcoholics tend to be cautious and controlled people, often overcontrolled and inhibited (Tamerin and Neumann, 1974), and they express open hostility or anger towards the counselor less frequently than might be expected. Strong personal controls are only one factor inhibiting the expression of anger; sober alcoholics are further deterred by their perception of the counselor's superior status, their need for the counselor's approval, and their fear of rejection. This by no means suggests that alcoholic clients rarely feel anger, but rather that their anger is most likely to be expressed in an indirect manner. Therefore, the counselor must be able to cope with the infrequent direct expressions of anger, and also be aware of cues suggesting disguised, controlled, or displaced anger.

Variables to Consider
1. sources of hostility towards the counselor
2. counselor-induced hostility
3. hostility as a therapeutic tool
4. disguised anger
5. displaced anger

Direct expressions of anger may occur as early as the first session, and are most frequent in coerced clients who feel angry even before meeting the counselor. Though angry remarks might be directed towards the counselor, typically they would have been expressed towards *any* intervenor. Such remarks as "I don't want your help," "This is a waste of time," or even "You can take your therapy and shove it!" are not so much attacks upon the counselor as they are reactions to the frustration of being coerced into treatment. Anger at the coercer has been displaced towards a less threatening object, the counselor.

43

8. Clients' Hostility

It is most important for the counselor to try to remain composed (remembering that the real object of the anger is someone or something else) and to permit clients to ventilate without interruption — with the possible exception of "I can appreciate your anger." Attempting to pacify clients is usually futile, and there is no great need to do so anyway. Indeed, the fact that the counselor has responded without disapproval may be the deciding factor in whether clients are willing to return. As previously noted, there is a high drop-out rate among angry, coerced clients, but the author has observed that such clients who do return are usually overly apologetic in the following session.

Another source of hostility in clients is their own feelings of helplessness and dependency (Roebuck and Kessler, 1972). One of the more frequently observed phenomena among alcoholics is their strong need for dependence (Catanzaro, 1968). Some alcoholic clients, unable to accept their heavy reliance on the counselor, become increasingly angry at him or her, while at the same time repressing their dependency needs. This behavior is identifiable as reaction-formation (expressing the opposite of the real feeling) in that the anger is usually way out of proportion, and seemingly unrelated, to any anger-producing events. Such clients have a fairly high drop-out rate, although many, due to their need for dependence on others, are likely to return.

Some alcoholic clients, as observed by Milt (1967), tend to be highly aggressive and prone to hostile behavior as a basic personality trait employed to ward off relationships with others. They usually start off aggressively in treatment and continue with the behavior. Milt places such clients in the poor prognosis category, as he considers a positive therapeutic relationship essential in the treatment of alcoholics.

We have just examined some instances of hostility displaced towards the counselor. Much more often, however, clients' direct hostility is either related to the interaction with the counselor or is unwittingly or even purposely induced by the counselor. According to Haymen (1966), reaction-formation can be provoked by the counselor relating to clients in an authoritarian manner; dependent clients who are experiencing conflict over their dependency needs may, in effect, be pushed into "rebellion." Negative feelings and hostile behavior by the counselor, too, may lead to defensiveness and retaliatory hostility by clients (Bandura et al., 1960). Other common sources of counselor-induced hostility are: making flippant remarks or taking too lightly serious concerns expressed by clients (what the counselor views as significant may be at variance with clients' immediate concerns); treating the underlying psychodynamics at the expense of symptom management (which is often very much at odds with clients' expectations); premature, excessive, or unrealistic demands (including ill-timed remarks such as criticizing clients' behavior without having established a climate of trust); frustration-producing behavior (e.g. often keeping clients waiting); monopolizing communications (compelling clients to remain passive); rejecting clients' interpretations (suggesting "I am the expert, not you!"); being nondirective when direction is called for (leaving clients dangling); making judgmental pronouncements about the "right way to live" (as contrasted with the current behavior and lifestyles of clients); appearing disinterested or preoccupied with other matters; and making promises or setting goals that realistically cannot be met.

Another significant source of hostility in clients is transference, a phenomenon that is difficult to research but commonly observed. Expressed in psychoanalytic terms, which place heavy emphasis on childhood experiences, transference is the projecting or investing of strong emotions that have been repressed in childhood onto the counselor. A classical example is the client with repressed angry feelings about authority figures (e.g. father) reacting with hostility to the counselor, whose perceived high status is equated with authority. But in less insight-oriented treatment approaches, if transference occurs, it is usually more superficial and less difficult to work with. If often relates more to "here and now events" in clients' lives than to early childhood experiences. Thus, expressions of hostility relating to the perceived status of the counselor may in fact indicate the inability to express anger in other areas of life, e.g. towards the boss or spouse. Or, economically disadvantaged clients may react with hostility to the well-dressed, well-paid counselor, because they perceive themselves as failures in comparison. Yet even in the less psychodynamic treatment approaches, transference can present a

8. Clients' Hostility

serious problem. Haymen (1966) notes that if treatment continues with no improvement in alcoholic clients, they may blame the counselor for their difficulties. In such cases, hostility and drop-out are to be expected, and not much can be done about it.

Whatever the source of clients' anger, its intensity and continuation seem to depend upon the response of the counselor. Both Haymen (1966) and Gamsky and Farwell (1966) report that hostile clients are rarely liked; their expressions of hostility towards the counselor usually evoke avoidance, disapproval, and antagonism in return. Bandura et al. (1960) and Berkowitz (1962) have found that "approaching" (directly responding to) clients' hostility may lead to further expressions of hostility; avoiding direct hostility, on the other hand, either discourages it or leads to a change in the object of hostility (Bandura et al., 1960).

It appears, then, that the counselor must be able to do three important things when working with hostile clients:

1. to objectify clients' anger, that is, not to feel personally threatened by it,
2. to respond effectively, and
3. to accept that the hostility is justified if it has been induced by the counselor.

The latter two abilities depend upon the first: when the counselor remains unrattled by clients' hostility, he or she can respond more effectively and can objectively consider whether the hostility might be justified. If, however, the counselor responds with avoidance and disapproval, the real source of the hostility can neither be identified nor worked out, which lets the counselor "off the hook" and leaves clients with no resolution to their anger. The message is, "It's okay to be angry as long as I'm not the object," and the anger then becomes suppressed or redirected.

There is a risk in "approaching" which the counselor should be prepared for: attempting to deal with clients' anger may temporarily produce more anger. Evidence suggests that for counselors who have a strong need for client approval, this reaction will cause considerable difficulty (Bandura et al., 1960). But as reported by Bruch (1974), the counselor's *usefulness* lies in his or her ability to react in an objective, unretaliatory way to angry attacks and with a readiness to explore the sources of the aggressive reaction. Wolberg (1967) takes the subject one step further, suggesting that verbal hostility should be accepted, discussed, and even encouraged. Treating alcoholic clients is not a "tea party" with rules calling for polite behavior only. That alcoholics are typically over-controlled and inhibited when sober is all the *more* reason for the counselor to attach considerable significance to hostile behavior.

In the author's experience, the risk involved in expressing hostility is far greater for clients than for the counselor, because clients may have to face loss or rejection. For example, a client in group therapy felt he was being "slighted" by the author. At the urging of his doctor, who occasionally served as a co-counselor in the group, the client prepared to express his anger. For two nights prior to the session he was unable to sleep, throughout the session he had nothing to say but was clearly agitated, and he only risked a confrontation — somewhat fearfully — after the other group members had left. His anger was at first meek and without much punch, yet when the author responded with interest and genuine concern, the intensity of the anger gradually increased until the client was almost shouting. The client had made his point success-fully: he was angry about the way he was being treated! When the author reassured him that he appreciated his feelings and very much wanted him to continue in treatment, the client remarked that if he had not said what had been on his mind, he probably would have gone home and "gotten drunk." This client's self-esteem was enhanced and his ability to be more assertive in later counseling sessions improved. As far as the "counselor's need for client approval" is concerned, after his outburst the client responded much more favorably to the author; expressing his anger allowed the release of his resentment. And that is a very important point. The expression of hostility, if accepted and handled appropriately by the counselor, clears the air and often improves the therapeutic relationship.

However, the chances to explore open hostility are rela-tively infrequent in alcoholism treatment. More often, anger at the counselor is disguised or displaced. When it is disguised, it usually takes the form of attempting to elicit annoyance or frustration from the counselor. Although these attempts may succeed temporarily, the behavior has a "boomerang" effect in the long run, with such clients being the real losers — *unless* the counselor has the insight to recognize the true motivation. A client may attempt to frustrate the counselor by showing up late for sessions; failing that, by canceling appointments at the last minute; and failing that, by neither showing nor canceling. Finally the frustrated counselor discharges the client. In effect, counselor and client have failed each other, the client having purposely acted irresponsibly and the counselor probably having misinterpreted the disguised anger as "poor motivation."

There are three possible explanations for a pattern or succession of client behaviors that frustrate the counselor, particularly when clients know the behaviors are having an effect: disguised anger, inappropriate motivation, and resistance to treatment. "Resistance to treatment" is a wastebasket term which is probably identical to "inappropriate motivation," as both terms suggest that clients feel little concern over whether the counselor is frustrated. Clients with disguised anger, however, are very aware of the effects of their behavior. Thus, the inappropriately motivated client may continue to arrive late irrespective of how the counselor responds, while the angry client will drop the behavior if it is not producing the desired reaction and in all likelihood will employ a new strategy.

Although the counselor may correctly identify behavior as disguised anger, bringing the anger out into the open and working with it may present real difficulties. Often clients who have a strong need to disguise their anger are not conscious of the connection between their attempts to frustrate the counselor and their anger towards the counselor. Indeed, they may find feelings of anger so unacceptable that the anger is not consciously experienced. Thus, they may feel somewhat pleased at having annoyed or frustrated the counselor, without knowing why this has given them pleasure.

The author has observed that such clients are typically very passive individuals who, when sober, rarely if ever express direct anger. Not only is the expression of anger disguised in the counseling setting, but in almost all other aspects of their lives as well. Often, in their childhoods, there were strong sanctions against expressing anger, and these early experiences became incorporated into their adult personalities. Such clients report that only seldom, if at all, do they feel conscious anger, and that the experience is usually quite upsetting and anxiety-provoking. Yet often, after drinking heavily, they may express intense feelings of anger, which in turn lead to guilt when sober.

Because these clients have little or no conscious awareness of their anger, confrontation and interpretation are most inappropriate. But the problem must be dealt with in some manner, as the behavior seriously disrupts the treatment process. A more general approach is recommended, commencing with assertiveness training, which helps passive clients to begin to "get in touch" with their feelings and not to withdraw from situations that demand assertive responses. (Assertiveness training for alcoholic clients is described in detail in Miller and Mastria, 1977: 63-81.)

There is also value in utilizing role-playing situations that in the beginning require minimal responses of annoyance, such as being shortchanged by a clerk or treated rudely by a telephone operator. If clients have difficulty expressing anger even when the situation is relatively benign, they can be directed to imagine an angry response without attempting to express it. *Very gradually,* as such clients learn to express anger in low-threat role playing, the counselor increases the degree of threat to situations such as being ignored by a salesperson or reacting to a friend who is unnecessarily very late for an appointment. The purpose of the role playing is to teach clients that the direct expression of anger, when appropriate, does not lead to dire consequences.

A common and highly visible response to this training is that, like children mastering a new skill, clients may begin to express anger "all over the place." This is a phase that passes as they learn to discriminate instances where the expression of anger is appropriate and where it is not. But the counselor must keep in mind that moving from disguise to direct expression is a slow and painstaking process.

When such clients are able to express anger somewhat more effectively, the counselor might attempt to direct their attention to their feelings about the counselor. (Sometimes this occurs spontaneously, but more often it requires prompting.) This can be a threatening experience, but if carefully trained and not asked to express their feelings prematurely, many clients do take the risk.

The counselor might begin by asking, "If you could change anything about *me*, what would you choose?" or "What about *me* do you sometimes find annoying?" Clearly, these questions do not require emotional outbursts, and if they are couched as genuine requests for corrective information, clients should be able to respond honestly. Realistically, however, it is a difficult task to replace deeply entrenched pathological behaviors with a more appropriate and effective repetoire of responses, and some clients may make only limited progress.

Displaced anger is in some respects easier to work with than disguised anger, because displacing clients are able to consciously experience anger and often to express it strongly. However, because the anger is not consciously directed towards the real object, in this case the counselor, detecting displaced anger may prove difficult. For example, a client who expresses hostility towards counselors in general may lead the counselor on a "wild goose chase," attempting to understand the client's feelings without being aware that he or she is the real object of the anger.

There is one useful rule of thumb that often helps in determining whether clients' anger at the counselor is being displaced: *the object of the displaced anger frequently relates to the treatment situation in some way.* The counselor should be on the alert for complaints about the office furniture, criticism of the receptionist, annoyance about the inconvenience of the scheduled appointment time, difficulties in arranging for transportation, complaints about prescribed medication, and general comments that counselors are overpaid, "crazier" than their clients, insensitive, and so on. Clients may stick with the same object for several sessions, or may find something new to criticize each week, but the theme of anger about *something* related to the treatment situation tends to remain constant. The keys to displaced anger are the repetition of complaints, anger that is out of proportion to the object, and overly solicitous behavior towards the counselor — the unconscious avoidance of any reference to the counselor that might suggest underlying hostility.

When the object(s) of anger are obviously related in some manner to the treatment situation, detection of displacement is made easier. But more subtle or remotely related objects cause greater difficulties in detection and may be overlooked by even a highly experienced counselor. For clients who see their counselor as an authority figure, hostility may be displaced onto the police, the employer, or even the government. But even here the same keys apply: repetition, out-of-proportion anger towards the object, and an overly solicitous attitude towards the counselor.

Displaced anger is less overtly disruptive to treatment than disguised anger. Covertly, however, it can interfere considerably. The disruptive potential is present even though it is harder to observe. Overly solicitous behavior, for example, is artificial and does not represent such clients' true feelings towards the counselor. Therefore, displacement cannot help but interfere with the development of a positive treatment relationship.

In addition, despite a high degree of superficial cooperation, clients' repressed hostile feelings are likely to undermine the counselor's goals and expectations. Such clients typically express willingness to go along with the counselor's recommendations, but something always seems to "get in the way" of successfully following through, and whatever that something is may then become an object of displaced anger. For example, after relapse a displacing client may complain, "I tried hard, but my spouse really upset me." The client is overly apologetic about letting the counselor down and simultaneously attacks the spouse vehemently, even though in reality the spouse's provocations might have been quite mild. The unconscious anger towards the counselor (possibly after a particularly upsetting session) may well have precipitated the relapse, but blame cannot consciously be directed towards the counselor; instead, it is directed towards a less threatening object, the spouse.

8. Clients' Hostility

Dealing with displaced anger once it is detected is one of the few areas in alcoholism treatment where the author has found insight and interpretation to be helpful, particularly with bright clients. Displacing clients already have the conscious ability to experience anger, and, provided the object of the anger is not too threatening, they may learn to express their feelings directly and appropriately. Unlike those individuals who resort to disguise in almost all upsetting situations, displacers are selective; their behavior is less pervasive and pathological.

In order for clients to respond to interpretation, the counselor must use a low-key approach, combining objectivity with genuine concern for the emotional impact the interpretation may have. The counselor must introduce the subject at a proper time, such as shortly after an expression of displaced anger, and might begin with a remark to set the stage: "I've noticed that there are some things that make you very angry, and I think it would be helpful for us to spend some time discussing your anger." That could be followed with: "I've been aware that you never seem to be angry at me, and I'd like to share my impressions about that with you." Proceeding gradually, the counselor might point out those objects and circumstances that appear to provoke anger, and how the client seems to avoid getting angry at the counselor: "Sometimes I've said and done things I thought might cause you to be annoyed with me, but that didn't happen." Asking clients for their opinions when they are not consciously feeling angry is of little value, for the response would probably take the form of "Well, I just don't feel any anger towards you." Instead, the counselor should interpret to clients why they might be having difficulties experiencing anger towards the counselor: e.g. *some people* find it very hard to express anger towards a counselor because they might be concerned about how the counselor will react; sometimes they won't even permit themselves to *experience* the anger, let alone *express* it; it's hard for some people to feel anger towards a person who is trying to help them, even though it is sometimes quite appropriate to feel that way; some people are afraid that the counselor won't like them if they get angry. The counselor might conclude, "I suspect that those are some of the reasons why you might find it hard to get angry at me even when I deserve it."

Because deep and symbolic interpretations generally aid clients very little in understanding the causes of their behavior, the interpretation should be kept simple. Indeed, interpretations rarely bring about changes in behavior unless they are combined with activities designed to elicit the desired behavior. Thus, immediately after the interpretation, when clients are focusing on the desired behavior and may now have some understanding of why it has not previously occurred, they should be led into imagining a situation where they might feel angry at the counselor. Although this exercise might be difficult at first, as any new behavior would be, it should not be impossible now that the threat value of the counselor has likely been reduced through the interpretation.

After the imaginary acting out, role playing should be undertaken to bring displacing clients closer to reality. The counselor sets up artificial situations, such as aggressively criticizing clients for some trivial behavior or completely ignoring concerns that clients believe to be important. Once such clients are able to express direct anger through role playing, displacement, at least in the treatment setting, tends to be dramatically reduced or even ceases.

9
Overt but Diffuse Anger

There is no literature or systematic research pertaining to this subject.

Angry alcoholic clients are likely to have had a long history of frustration, rejection, and anxiety-producing experiences, usually beginning in childhood. Unlike blaming alcoholics, who have little difficulty identifying the sources of their hostility (however misdirected they may be), alcoholics whose anger is diffuse have usually experienced such a variety of rejecting and frustrating situations that they are unable to specify any definite causes; their anger is often expressed in an intellectualized, vague, and inappropriately directed manner. Initially, the counselor is bombarded with such a montage of anger towards the world, society, people, social injustice, and so on, that it seems difficult to respond with anything more than listening in an accepting and sympathetic manner.

In the early phases of treatment such clients usually show less interest in their alcohol problems than in proving to the counselor that the world is hostile, uncaring, and insensitive. At hand, they have overwhelming evidence to support their feelings: millions of starving people, war, exploitation, the selfish aims of others, poverty, and oppressive governments. The author recalls an alcoholic client whose major preoccupation was with the decimation of whales. At the slightest provocation he would angrily denounce governments for condoning such slaughter and people for using whale products.

Often the attitude of such clients towards themselves is that life has dealt them a "dirty deal," and that they are the victims of circumstances far beyond their control. They often conclude, "No wonder I've resorted to alcohol."

55

9. Overt Anger

Variables to Consider
1. diffuse anger as a "smoke screen" for aloneness and helplessness
2. caution by the counselor; the low-key therapeutic relationship
3. encouraging social involvement and outlets for anger

Clients with diffuse hostility are usually single, have few, if any, friends and no strong emotional attachments; if employed, they typically express considerable dissatisfaction with their jobs; they either reject or more likely have been rejected by their families; and they engage in practically no rewarding activities, with the possible exception of brief "flings" with organizations concerned with social issues. They are likely to describe themselves as loners who believe that people cannot be trusted, and others often view them as "peculiar" or "strange." They drink alone, usually at home.

Intellectualized and diffuse anger is a "smoke screen" which, combined with alcohol, serves to prevent such clients from experiencing the traumatic realities of their own lives — to protect them from the helplessness and loneliness that they feel they can do nothing about. If they have had emotional involvements with others in the past, they invariably made poor choices, which only reinforced their angry retreat from the world. Insulation from others has become necessary to avoid further hurt and rejection. Alcohol is a comforting "friend" that soothes, assists in the life-style of avoidance, and provides temporary relief from the feelings of helplessness.

The counselor should exercise caution when working with such clients. Psychological evaluation should be undertaken, as the adjustment pattern *may* indicate schizophrenia. In any event, these clients' overly cautious approach to people extends to the counselor as well, and at least during the early phase of treatment their willingness to attend sessions may depend upon the counselor's ability to maintain emotional distance. Direct overtures such as "I do care about you," or "You can trust me," should be avoided. Caring is better demonstrated through concerned interest, nonconfrontation, and noninterpretation. These clients should be viewed as potentially high-risk individuals who, if faced with psychodynamic interpretations of themselves, may become increasingly hostile or seriously depressed. The counselor must keep in mind that such clients believe they can relate to others only through angry communications; anger is their reality, protecting them from both a hostile world and inner turmoil.

During the early phases of counseling it is desirable to wean these clients gradually from using all of the treatment time for expressions of diffuse anger, and to begin concentrating on alcohol abuse. Complete weaning, however, will not be accomplished for some time. Because the only positive reinforcement these clients receive for regular attendance may be the counselor's interested listening, removing the reinforcer too early may remove the incentive to attend. The weaning process is, in effect, an unstated bargain: "I am willing to spend some of our time listening to you provided we also spend some time working on your alcohol problem." Concrete homework assignments such as keeping a daily drinking log, recording feelings, personal contacts, and the use of free time throughout each day may provide topics for discussion in weekly meetings and at the same time help clients to focus on concerns other than their anger.

After a few sessions of respecting clients' needs for emotional distance, the counselor should begin to make warm but low-key remarks such as "I'm glad to see you today," and "I feel good about our session today." Clients' reactions to such remarks will guide the counselor in increasing the intensity of "feeling statements." Praise for abstinence and other appropriate behaviors also helps reinforce the therapeutic relationship. (The author has observed that over a period of time such clients come to expect expressions of praise and personal warmth.) Slowly, they are learning that it is possible for someone to care about them, and in this instance they are unlikely to be rejected. To accomplish this important goal, the counselor must take care to avoid negative remarks about inappropriate behavior. If a constructive discussion is possible, it should be pursued; if not, the counselor should make no response at all.

9. Overt Anger

As clients begin to appear more comfortable and responsive to the counselor's recommendations, engaging in other low-risk interpersonal situations should be encouraged. AA is often useful because it helps to maintain clients' focus on abstinence and requires some minimal social involvement.

Long-range planning with clients of this type must be realistic. They may never give up their anger entirely — nor is it necessary that they do so — but may learn to bring it under enough control to become involved in rewarding activities. Instead of attempting to extinguish the anger, the counselor may have more success in redirecting it towards social and/or environmental issues. Such clients may already be fringe members of social action groups; increasing their involvement can provide a level of interpersonal contact that is comfortable to them, as well as a constructive outlet for their continuing anger. In addition to AA and continued treatment, such activities may prove effective in controlling clients' alcoholism, increasing their level of self-esteem, and counteracting their feelings of helplessness.

10
Serious Psychopathology

There is little reference in the literature to psychopathology in alcoholics, but the outpatient staff at the Addiction Research Foundation's Clinical Institute rated it as a serious disrupter of treatment. Several factors may account for the under-discussion of this issue.

Many socially isolated alcoholics do not come to the attention of treatment agencies. Their only contacts in the helping professions may be with physicians for strictly medical problems or with welfare workers who may be inadequately trained. Although seriously disturbed alcoholics are well represented in the "skid row" population, they are usually known only to police or hospital emergency department staff, who view their own responsibility as immediate management. Since alcohol may mask other psychopathological symptoms and afford at least minimal opportunity to function, seriously disturbed alcoholics are unlikely to seek treatment on their own. Still others may be overprotected by their families, who encourage continued dependency and further drinking (Wilson, 1968). Even if disturbed alcoholics are provided with treatment, it is virtually impossible to assess the underlying pathology as long as they are continuing to drink (Curlee, 1971). Finally, alcoholics with personality or character disorders (e.g. asocial personality, sociopath) practically never, in the author's experience, seek treatment on their own. Thus, deeply disturbed alcoholics are only occasionally treated for alcoholism as outpatients.

Variables to Consider
1. psychological assessment
2. counseling vs. referral to a psychiatrist

It is the author's opinion that in addition to a history, a

brief psychological assessment should be taken of all clients. (Senior staff are assumed to be training and supervising students and less experienced counselors in assessment techniques.)

With the exception of "denying" (Section 1) and "blaming" (Section 11) alcoholics, all clients should be requested to abstain from alcohol during treatment because only then can any underlying pathology be assessed. If fairly objective and valid pencil and paper psychological tools such as the Minnesota Multiphasic Personality Inventory (MMPI) are employed under qualified supervision, the counselor can often obtain a useful profile of existing psychopathology. Despite the inconvenience to some clients and the drawbacks of "using a big net to catch a few fish," assessment is well worth the time because early planning can reduce the probability of having to contend with serious disruptive or acting-out problems later.

History-taking in conjunction with psychological tests often provides pertinent information such as previous psychiatric treatment, hospitalization, arrest history, poor social and sexual adjustment, poor work history, and history of violent or suicidal behavior. Mendelson (1966) describes interview assessment techniques for alcoholics, but these are time-consuming, must be carried out by very experienced counselors, and there is no evidence that the results are more valid than those of objective psychological tests.

Even without psychological testing, if psychiatric disturbance is evident or even suspected, the counselor should seek guidance from a senior staff person before developing any treatment plan. Some broad guidelines are recommended. If a client appears to be psychotic, abstinence *may* provoke an acute psychotic reaction. Immediate referral to a psychiatrist for evaluation for possible hospitalization is highly recommended.

According to both Milt (1967) and Dielthelm (1955), some sociopaths begin drinking at an early age, becoming confirmed alcoholics in their early twenties. Due to their high potential for acting out when both sober and drunk, such individuals are poor treatment risks. The major problem so often encountered with this diagnostic group is their apparent inability to profit from experience; although they may be superficially cooperative, they typically undermine the best efforts of even highly experienced counselors. Such clients have commonly been coerced into treatment by legal authorities and tend to drop out as soon as coercion is relaxed. Caution is advised in accepting this type of client for treatment. If accepted, clients must agree to stringent controls, including the release of attendance information to parole or probation officers and the use of a "protective" drug such as Antabuse.

Clinical decisions regarding moderately to severely depressed alcoholics should be made with care. As suicidal behavior is not uncommon among seriously depressed alcoholics, such clients should be referred to a psychiatrist for inpatient treatment. Don't gamble! The risk is too great (Jacobs, 1975). Moderate depression due to numerous failures and low self-esteem is often observed in alcoholics (Chafetz, 1959). Here, supportive therapy is essential and antidepressant medication may prove effective, but should be provided only if clients are abstaining from alcohol.

Some individuals with severe neurotic anxiety reactions resort to alcohol for relief. Often they experience increased anxiety and considerable guilt as a result of their drinking behavior, which may motivate them to seek assistance. They are typically quite dependent, and during the early phases of treatment may require more than one visit per week (Mendelson, 1966). Tranquillizing medication, *carefully monitored*, is often helpful during the first several weeks of abstinence. Since anxiety is such a common symptom among alcoholics, a differential diagnosis of neurosis is often made on the basis of the magnified guilt such clients experience both in regard to their drinking and to other aspects of their lives. If relapses occur frequently and medication has been ineffective or abused, hospitalization should be seriously considered.

Chronic alcoholics (those who have a long history of regular alcohol abuse) are subject to organic brain damage, most obviously manifested in short-term memory impairment (inability to recall relatively recent events), confusion, inability to care for their basic needs, reduced ability to reason abstractly, and in some instances bizarre visual hallucinations. If any of these and other peculiarities in behavior are evident, immediate referral to a physician is mandatory.

11

Blaming

With the exception of paranoid individuals, no other people contend so strongly that their difficulties are caused by problems outside of their control than is the case with certain alcoholics. After listening to clients angrily lament their plights, it is sometimes tempting to remark, "It's about time you stopped kidding yourself." However, this reponse is most ill-advised, particularly in the early sessions. Often such clients have been pressured into treatment, but retain an entrenched belief in their innoncence — "I wouldn't have an alcohol problem if my wife would just stop nagging me or if my boss would just get off my back, or if people would just leave me alone."

To one experienced clinician (Wolberg, 1967), "blaming" clients, whether or not their problems relate to alcohol, are among the most difficult to treat. Blaming alcoholics believe they cannot be held responsible for their drinking, and expect sympathy and understanding from the counselor. They may genuinely believe, for example, that it is their *spouses,* not themselves, who should be receiving treatment, and will repeat this theme again and again. Understandably, and contrary to such clients' expectations, the counselor experiences frustration and annoyance.

Variables to Consider
1. blaming vs. excusing
2. psychodynamics of blaming clients
3. neutrality and noninterpretation by the counselor
4. fostering clients' personal responsibility; timing

Blaming clients should be distinguished from those who give excuses for their continued drinking. The latter are generally less hostile, less disturbed, and better able to see the spurious relationship between their drinking and the manufactured excuse.

11. Blaming

In addition, after the excuse has been eliminated (through conjoint therapy, job change, learning to relax, etc.) they are ultimately more willing to accept that their drinking is a self-perpetuating behavior, and to recognize that searching for another excuse would be self-deceptive.

Blaming alcoholics, in contrast, tend to project blame for anything that goes wrong in their lives onto others or onto circumstances they cannot control, often lack insight into their inappropriate behavior, tend to exaggerate minor incidents in order to support the blaming behavior, have little difficulty finding new targets for blaming once the original source has been eliminated, are deeply suspicious of the motives of others, and are often prone to aggressive, even violent, behavior when drinking.

When working with blaming clients, it is imperative that throughout treatment the counselor remain noninterpretative and neutral regarding the blaming behavior. This is indeed a difficult task, and to accomplish it the counselor should keep the unconscious psychodynamics in mind. Individuals who project blame onto others have repressed feelings of responsibility for personally unacceptable behavior (e.g. heavy alcohol consumption); they are unable to allow themselves to consciously admit that their behavior is wrong. Therefore, if they engage in the unacceptable behavior, they must find a consciously acceptable reason for doing so. Blaming an external source for "driving me to drink" permits such individuals to continue the unacceptable behavior because there is now a good (conscious) reason for doing so. This accounts for the frequent unwillingness of blaming alcoholics to leave their spouses or even to agree to conjoint therapy: the blamer must have someone or something to blame. (However, as previously noted, even if the object of blame is removed [e.g. the spouse leaves], these alcoholics usually have little difficulty in finding new sources to blame.) Such clients often try to convince the counselor that the spouse purposely instigates upsetting situations in order to compel the blamer to drink. The author has often heard arguments such as "She really *wants* me to drink so that she can have a reason for being angry and making me feel miserable. Then she can do what she wants without feeling guilty, because I'm drunk." Blamers are unaware that most often they themselves have been the instigators.

Thus, the need to remain noninterpretative and neutral about the blaming behavior becomes clear. If the counselor attempts to point out that the blaming behavior is not valid, such clients are very likely to terminate treatment and to incorporate into their distorted belief system the conviction that the counselor just doesn't understand.

On the other hand, sympathy on the part of the counselor for these clients' predicaments (e.g. having such a "bad guy" for a spouse) in effect supports the clients' reasons for continuing to drink. Treatment must be directed towards the symptom and its control; it must not slip into endless discussions of the blaming and fruitless attempts to interpret the behavior to clients.

The author recalls a client who directly attributed her drinking to her husband's constant criticism. He left, and public housing and mothers' allowance were arranged. The husband was gone, but the drinking continued, with the blame merely being transferred to the "poor housing conditions" and "loneliness." The author did not tamper with the client's defenses; instead he suggested that in spite of "what she had to put up with," she was only hurting herself by continuing to drink, and that it would be quite an accomplishment on her part if she could quit drinking even with the continuing external pressures. In effect, she was given a "license" to continue her blaming (which she would have done in any event), but was also asked to take responsibility by doing something that was in her best interest. The author neither approved nor disapproved of her blaming behavior; he merely accepted it as an overriding personality trait around which he would have to work. What the client had to gain was increased self-respect and personal pride.

Timing is important in asking blaming clients to take responsibility for changing their drinking behavior, as it may take them some time to conclude that the counselor presents no real threat. The counselor accepts, neither condemning nor condoning. In fact, accepting the reality that certain behaviors, like blaming, are highly resistant to change makes it less frustrating to work with such clients and enhances the possibility of a positive counseling relationship. When clients recognize that, as well as being no threat, the counselor is sincerely interested in their well-being, they are more likely to be responsive to recommendations.

Blaming alcoholics typically have very poor prognoses; they are their own worst enemies, caught up in a vicious circle of blaming, then drinking which leads to further blaming, then further drinking, and so on. But a patient counselor may be able to have an impact by dealing with the symptom instead of concentrating on the underlying psychopathology.

12

Frequent Lateness for Appointments

While this problem is very common among alcoholic clients, there is no literature or systematic research relating to it.

Although counselor and client may have agreed that it is the client's responsibility to arrive on time for appointments, certain clients are consistently late. Given that only a small fraction of the week is set aside for each client, it is necessary to use the maximum time available. Frequent lateness is frustrating for the counselor, as it is valuable time wasted. Therefore, addressing the issue should not be postponed.

Variables to Consider
1. lateness as a testing behavior
2. lateness in a disorganized lifestyle
3. lateness in resistant clients
4. counselor responses

In the case of testing clients (who may be attempting to determine how permissive the counselor can be), a simple, detached confrontation should be tried first: "This is the second consecutive week you've been late. It's cutting into the limited time we have to spend together. So please make a greater effort to be on time." This serves notice to clients that the counselor does not react permissively to lateness, and in some instances may be enough to bring about change.

Other testing clients may need firmer controls. The counselor might choose, for example, not to see clients on any occasion when they are more than 10 minutes late unless there is a valid excuse. Latecomers are merely given a new appointment for the following week. Some may view this as a rather strong measure, but if the repeated lateness is sufficiently frustrating

12. Frequent Lateness

to the counselor that it becomes disruptive to treatment, the behavior must be brought under control. It has been the author's experience that while clients may initially react quite negatively to such a control, the testing behavior ceases rapidly. And, instead of detracting from the therapeutic relationship, it is likely to enhance it: the counselor is no longer frustrated with the client, and the client has learned that the counselor will, if pressed, respond with firm controls, which relieves the client of the need to continue testing.

A more common and less desirable approach is: "It's your hour and if you want to waste part of it, that's up to you." This both suggests to clients that the expectations of the counselor need not be met and permits irresponsible behavior to continue without correction, thus increasing the likelihood of future irresponsible behavior.

Lateness can result from factors other than testing, such as a disorganized lifestyle. This source is easily differentiated from testing behavior in that disorganized individuals exhibit patterns of inconsistency in many aspects of their lives. Such clients must be handled in a direct and concrete manner. Explicit information is necessary: "What do you usually do on the day of your appointment?" "Where are you just before you come here?" "How long does it take you to get here?" "What are some of the things that interfere with your getting here on time?" In order to help such clients regularly arrive on time, the counselor might instruct them, for example, to telephone the receptionist, no matter what they are doing, one hour prior to the appointment to confirm that they will be on time. If no contact has been made, the receptionist then calls them and cancels the scheduled appointment, offering a future appointment and reminding them of the responsibility to call in advance. Canceling the appointment is in the best interests of both counselor and clients. Instead of sitting and waiting, the counselor can now use the free time for other business. For clients, the cancelation is likely to produce frustration, which can only be avoided in the future by being more attentive to what is expected. At least in this aspect of such clients' lives there may be some organization!

Training disorganized clients to develop schedules, to be aware of time, to break away from time-wasting activities, etc. may require as much session time as working on their alcohol problems. But because disorganization typically results in feelings of frustration, the effort is well worthwhile. Improved organization *may* be directly translated into improved control over alcohol use, as it is quite possible that one of the functions of alcohol has been to relieve the tension produced by frustration.

There is one case where, in the author's opinion, it may not be desirable to take any specific action regarding lateness: the resistant client. More often than not, resistant clients have been pressured into treatment; they are negative, angry, and only superficially cooperative. Their expectations regarding treatment are typically low. During the early sessions with such clients, the counselor's major goal should be to develop an accepting relationship. Eliciting an agreement to attend sessions regularly may be all that can be realistically expected, and any other reasonable demands should be postponed. Thus, temporary lateness should be ignored in favor of appreciation that such clients have shown up at all. The subject of lateness should only be broached after resistant clients have demonstrated their willingness to work on their alcohol problems. Pressuring such clients too early will probably lead to drop-out.

13

Frequent Telephone Calls when Drinking or Distressed

If the counselor makes it clear from the beginning that it is not appropriate for clients to call while intoxicated, then the counselor must stand firm. Telephoning under such conditions is a violation of that agreement. In the author's experience, the caller is usually testing the counselor's tolerance — his or her willingness to put up with unacceptable behavior.

Variables to Consider
1. inappropriate responses by the counselor
2. recommended responses
3. overly dependent clients

If the counselor responds to calls from intoxicated clients with permissiveness, clients have learned that the counselor can be manipulated to disregard an agreement. In all likelihood the behavior will occur again, and the chances of clients testing the counselor in other matters of agreement will increase. Permissiveness, or the unwillingness to place controls on client behavior is rarely in the best interests of alcoholic clients, as it undermines the counselor's ability to help clients develop internal controls.

Another less than desirable approach is to concentrate on psychodynamics: to probe the underlying causes of the specific inappropriate behavior at the expense of attempting to eliminate it quickly. All too often this lets clients "off the hook;" it avoids the important issue of holding clients accountable for their own actions. Focusing on psychodynamics is, in effect, a form of permissiveness. It may even reinforce the behavior by elevating it to an object of serious study — which may be an interesting exercise but of little value in helping clients to stop the behavior.

13. Frequent Calls

In the long run, also, fruitless analyses may frustrate and anger the counselor (Steiner, 1969).

There are several responses to calls from intoxicated clients that may prove effective. By choosing not to accept the call at all, or by making it extremely brief, the counselor does not positively reinforce the behavior by listening. Clients may continue for a short time with such calls, but it probably will not take them long to learn that they gain nothing from the behavior, as it is being ignored. Behaviors that receive no positive reinforcement soon cease.

A second approach is to deal with the telephone calls in the next session in a neutral, terse, and unequivocal way. The counselor should confront such clients with a statement that their behavior is in violation of the agreement — little or nothing of value can be accomplished while clients are intoxicated. No discussion is required. It suffices to conclude, "Therefore I cannot accept your call when you have been drinking," and perhaps to add a positive incentive: "If you call when you're sober, though, I will attempt to make myself available."

A third approach is for the counselor to indicate his or her feelings about the calls, e.g. "It bothers me when you behave that way." This relatively mild expression of feeling (as opposed to "I will not tolerate such behavior!") enables clients to become aware of the consequences of their behavior: they have annoyed someone who cares about them. Role playing can be useful in underscoring the point. Reversing roles demonstrates to clients how they sound and behave when intoxicated and what emotional reactions they experience while serving in the role of counselor. This experience is often quite surprising to clients.

Finally, the counselor may choose to tape-record calls from intoxicated clients, playing the tape back during the next session. This action permits no doubt or misunderstanding; it is a dramatic demonstration to clients of their inappropriate behavior. In order to pursue this approach, the counselor has an ethical responsibility to inform clients in a neutral manner that the call is being taped, but in the author's experience, discharging this responsibility in no way affects the impact of the call at the next session.

There is no reason to assume that any one of the above suggestions will work with all clients, or that all four are equally effective in all situations. The choice of approach depends upon the nature of the counseling relationship and upon which suggestion the counselor feels most comfortable with.

Some clients may become frequent callers when distressed, even when they are sober. In some instances, accepting frequent calls may be appropriate rather than permissive. During the difficult transition between alcohol abuse and abstinence, some dependent clients require almost daily reassurance. As long as there are controls (e.g. no longer than a few minutes and at a time when the counselor is free), such calls may help certain clients to remain abstinent. There must be a *definite* understanding that these supportive calls will cease after a specified period of time, and to avoid any future misunderstanding, the details should be put in writing.

Frequent calls may also be acceptable under unusual circumstances, such as during a crisis or in order to maintain close contact with a potentially suicidal client. But here, too, controls are necessary.

In all other instances, frequent calls should be discouraged because they are likely to increase clients' dependence on the counselor. Indeed, in the case of overly dependent clients, a goal of treatment is improved self-reliance. Thus, reducing the frequency of telephone calls when such clients are distressed is a high priority. The counselor should insist that overly dependent clients keep careful logs of all distress-related calls to other helping professionals, friends, and relatives. These records should include clients' emotional state, the reason for calling, and the response of the person who is called. The logs may be reviewed in counseling sessions with the same question posed for each entry: "How could you have handled this on your own?" Initially, overly dependent clients may have difficulty responding to this question, and the counselor will have to do some active coaching in self-reliance training. But gradually, through the counselor's praise for self-developed strategies and clients' increased practice, the counselor will begin to play a more passive role and clients will need to make fewer distress-related calls.

14

Clients Arriving Drunk for Counseling

Although this is a relatively infrequent event in outpatient settings, the counselor should be prepared for it. Research on both primates (Fitzgerald, 1977) and humans (Boyatzis, 1975) suggests that aggressive behavior when under the influence of alcohol occurs most often in individuals who are aggressive when sober. Thus, observing clients' behavior when sober as well as knowing the history of their typical behaviors when drinking will provide the counselor with clues for what to anticipate *if* clients arrive in an intoxicated state.

Variables to Consider
1. handling passive, verbally aggressive, and physically aggressive clients
2. continuing counseling after the event

In the author's experience, the overwhelming majority of alcoholics who arrive for an appointment in an intoxicated state present no real threat. If they appear to be relatively passive, they should be taken aside, and in a gentle, friendly manner the counselor should suggest that it would be a good idea to forget the appointment, that the receptionist will call a cab, and that a new appointment will be made for the same time the following week. The counselor should avoid referring to the fact that clients are drunk or that their behavior is highly inappropriate, because this might cause manageable individuals to become less manageable. The counselor is advised to remain with such clients until the taxi arrives, possibly bringing them coffee and listening in a sympathetic manner.

More aggressive or angry intoxicated clients require an outwardly calm and unperturbed posture (even though the counselor may be "shaky" on the inside). The most important thing is to handle the immediate situation without incident. The counselor should take such clients to a quiet area but with the door left open and preferably with a third person present. Rather than directly questioning them about their condition, the counselor should offer supportive statements such as "I appreciate how you feel," or "That's very understandable," and should make reference to future contact, such as "I guess we're going to have to discuss that next time we meet." (This reassures clients that they will not necessarily be abandoned.) Throughout the encounter, the counselor should permit clients to do most of the talking and to "blow off steam," resisting the temptation to disagree, and treating clients with concern and respect. When such clients appear to be calming down, the counselor might say," A taxi is on the way and I'll stay here with you until it arrives."

Occasionally, intoxicated clients may direct angry remarks at the counselor but without any suggestion of physical threat. In this case, the above strategy should be followed with the addition of neutral remarks like "I'm sorry to hear that you feel that way," or "I hope we can sort things out." Attempts at debate or defense only tend to increase the intensity of the angry remarks.

Only very rarely do intoxicated clients present a direct physical threat. Such clients should *definitely not* be taken into an office. They should be seen in the waiting area because, as suggested by Kiraly (personal communication), the best deterrent against physical abuse is to have as many people around as possible. At all costs, the counselor should avoid retaliatory hostile remarks that might instigate violence, and should respond honestly: "You are frightening me. If you won't calm down I'll have to get help." If such clients continue in a threatening manner, someone outside the waiting area should telephone the police. If they do calm down, they should be asked to leave by a staff member *other* than the target of the hostility.

Should a counselor continue to work with clients who have arrived in an intoxicated state? With the exception of those who presented a direct physical threat, in most instances the answer is yes. If the anger directed towards the counselor was without any reference to physical threat, whether or how the counselor proceeds depends greatly upon how upsetting the experience was. If the counselor chooses not to continue, such a client should be contacted with an explanation, e.g. "I no longer feel comfortable working with you [this is a realistic consequence of the client's behavior], and I feel it is best for both of us that treatment be terminated."

Continuing to work with clients who arrived in an intoxicated state requires a firm understanding: it will not happen again! Clients should be advised that they are responsible for their behavior even when intoxicated. Therefore, if they are drinking prior to a future appointment, it is their responsibility to cancel the appointment. (This is a rare exception to the rule regarding telephoning while drinking.) Some counselors, in order to avoid a further occurrence, reschedule such clients for an early morning appointment. This strategy appears pointless as it merely requires clients to change their drinking schedules without exercising personal responsibility.

Arriving drunk for a counseling session may be a "graphic demonstration" of clients' unwillingness to seriously attempt to control their drinking. Or it may be a "lapse," albeit a serious one. But to overdramatize the single event is ill-advised; it is always possible that a client intended to "have a beer" and learned a painful lesson. As with a lapse, such clients should be given the benefit of the doubt unless future behavior proves otherwise. This approach should not be construed as excessive permissiveness because it is understood that a second occurrence will necessitate strong measures such as suspension of treatment or complete abstinence through Antabuse.

15

Intoxication Suspected

Probably more alcoholic clients arrive for treatment "under the influence" than counselors suspect. A single drink or even two can lead to such slight behavioral changes in many alcoholics that the event may easily go undetected. There is no reference made to this subject in the literature.

Variables to Consider
1. detection
2. counselor response
3. the questionable value of a drink before a session

When working with alcoholics, careful observation of clients' typical behavior is required — not only the obvious things, but the subtle as well: rate of speech, favored sitting posture, muscle tension, usual emotional state during interviews, attentiveness, expressions of feeling, degree of passivity or aggressiveness in response to the counselor, consistency of communication (as compared to frequent attempts to change the subject), usual subjects of communication, manner (friendly, aloof, negative, cooperative, etc.). Changes in any of the above may relate to events that occurred prior to the session. They may also have to do with the specific topic under discussion. Or, they *may* suggest that clients have been drinking.

In the early phases of treatment, when the counselor is getting to know clients and observing their behavior, there is not yet sufficient information to allow a response to relatively minor fluctuations in behavior. This can only occur later, when typical behaviors have been noted. Even if clients have not been drinking, responding to the above cues is often valuable. For example, "You appear to be a little uptight and preoccupied" is an appropriate lead in to discussing something that might be bothering a client.

15. Intoxication Suspected

Such a comment makes clients aware that the counselor is sensitive and interested, and it may even serve as a deterrent to drinking prior to a session, as the counselor has demonstrated his or her attentiveness to changes in typical behavior.

Whether or not the changes in behavior may be due to alcohol consumption, the counselor is advised to consider this possibility. If there is cause for suspicion, the situation can be handled with a minimum of "ruffled feathers." The following is one possible approach:

> Counselor: *You seem to be more relaxed, talkative, and open today.*
> Client: *I just feel good.*
> Counselor: *Is this the way you are when you've had a bit to drink?*

There is no accusation here, merely a reasonable question to elicit information. If the question is presented in a neutral manner (rather than "I'm suspicious of you"), sober clients will probably respond in a nondefensive way. Clients who may have had a few drinks are likely to assume the counselor is suspicious, and may become defensive. Or, due to guilt feelings, they may acknowledge that they did have something to drink before the appointment, If so, such clients should be informed, if an agreement has not already been reached, that it is their responsibility not to drink, and particularly not before a session. The point has been made, and the counselor should now move into another topic. If clients respond defensively, the counselor is best advised to drop the subject with an "Okay, I'll take your word for it." The message has been delivered without accusation, making such clients aware that their change in behavior was not overlooked, thus reducing the probability of its recurrence.

Some might argue that a drink or two may "loosen the tongue" and result in a profitable session. But what is the counselor to say at the end of the session? — "I condone your drinking today because we made progress, but I expect you to be completely sober next week." When clients are being treated for alcoholism, one can hardly ascribe "progress" to sessions occurring after they have been drinking, regardless of the content of those sessions. Part of the counseling process is to help alcoholics feel comfortable and to open up while sober. The counselor must be consistent.

16

Refusal to Take Medication

There is disagreement among alcoholism workers regarding Antabuse. Some believe that any drug that deters clients from drinking (due to the very unpleasant side effects) removes personal responsibility for abstinence; clients depend upon a "pill" instead of developing their own internal controls. Others believe that abstinence is a precondition for the development of internal controls, and thus are more likely to consider the use of Antabuse early in treatment. Still others believe that a drug should be used only when client and counselor agree that all other alternatives have been exhausted.

There is no firm evidence to support the superiority of any one of these approaches, but in the author's opinion the third alternative is the most reasonable. Clearly, it is best if clients can learn to abstain without resorting to medication, but in reality many alcoholics do require temporary pharmacological assistance, particularly when the only other way to bring about abstinence appears to be hospitalization. Antabuse is preferable to hospitalization because it causes minimum disruption in clients' lives and because clients can continue to work with the counselor on their drinking problems within the everyday environment that has helped maintain the behavior.

Variables to Consider
1. Antabuse as a crutch
2. clients' embarrassment
3. length of use; caution at cessation
4. reports from the spouse

Probably the most common objection to Antabuse is that it is a "crutch." It *is* a crutch; that is exactly what it was designed to be. After clients have attempted — and repeatedly failed — to abstain, the counselor should not ask, "Is this person motivated to quit?" A more appropriate question is, "How can I help make it less difficult for this client to abstain?"

The fact that clients may view Antabuse with disfavor does not necessarily suggest they are unmotivated to quit. Although this may be true in some instances, in others it is due to disappointment at having to accept a crutch. The already low self-esteem of some clients may well be further damaged (although usually only temporarily) by acknowledging that they cannot make it on their own and thus, once again, are failures. It is important for the counselor to recognize and be sensitive to these painful feelings. (Contending with the "crutch" argument is found in Section 2: "Continued Drinking while in Treatment.")

Although they may drink themselves into a stupor, some alcoholics totally reject the use of drugs, a fact of which they are proud. In working with such clients, the author has had some success by suggesting, "Possibly it would be a good idea to take the Antabuse for a while and be proud that you are not drinking." Since Antabuse is a last resort, if clients reject it, hospitalization or suspension of treatment should then be discussed. (Clients should be given a week or two to make the decision.) The counselor should not tolerate continued drinking for an indefinite period of time after Antabuse has been suggested.

Although this usually goes unrecognized, because clients rarely mention it, many alcoholics are simply embarrassed about going into a pharmacy — particularly one where they usually shop — with a prescription for Antabuse. They view the prescription as a "badge of dishonor," for the pharmacist can have no doubt as to why the medication is being prescribed. When recommending the regular use of Antabuse, the counselor should explore with clients their feelings about the pharmacist being aware of their alcoholism. If they can handle the situation, fine! But if they are sufficiently embarrassed, they might consider using a different pharmacy exclusively to fill the Antabuse prescription. The author suspects that embarrassment is one of the main reasons that clients "forget" to have their prescriptions filled.

Assuming clients accept Antabuse, for how long should it be prescribed? There are no specific guidelines in the literature, but the author has found that two or three months usually suffice for first-time users. For clients who have relapsed after termination of use, more extended periods may be required. In either case, use of the medication should be carefully supervised by the prescribing physician. In addition, the counselor must explain to clients (because some physicians do not) that since Antabuse builds up in the fatty tissues of the body, it is unwise to consume *any* alcohol for at least one week after termination (or risk suffering a decidedly unpleasant physical response). If at any time clients wish to stop taking Antabuse, it should be with the agreement of the counselor and on an experimental basis, with the understanding that the medication may have to be reinstituted at a later date.

Occasionally, a spouse will call to inform the counselor that a client is not taking the medication. This is *not* a desirable way to obtain information, no matter how useful it may be. The spouse should be advised to tell the client about the call before the next appointment, because at that time the counselor will have an obligation to discuss the content of the call with the client. Keeping the call secret would be a violation of trust. Perhaps, if the client approves, a discussion with both the client and the spouse would be appropriate at this juncture in order to clarify what, if any, contact the spouse should have with the counselor.

17

Game Playing

According to Steiner (1969), alcoholic clients are quite proficient at game playing. Throughout their drinking years most alcoholics have learned the art of deception (and falsely raising the hopes of others): continuing to drink while at the same time suggesting that quitting is just around the corner. It is no wonder that many have become very effective game players. Most frequently underlying their "gaming" in treatment are hostility, the need to control or manipulate the counselor, and avoidance of coming to terms with their alcoholism or other personal problems.

Game playing is among the most common disrupters to the treatment process and should never be tolerated, as it invariably distracts attention from the real treatment issues and engages the counselor in time-wasting and fruitless interactions with clients. Young counselors are particularly vulnerable because lack of experience makes it harder to detect and control game playing.

Variables to Consider
1. the con game
2. outwitting the counselor
3. purposeful misinterpretation
4. frequently changing the subject
5. intellectual discourses
6. unreasonable demands
7. flattery, praise, and gifts

The *con game* is one of the more popular and difficult-to-detect games at which some alcoholics are remarkably expert. At its roots is an attempt to lull the counselor into believing that all is well, everything is running smoothly, and (subtly) that the counselor is doing a fine job. In fact, when the con game is being played it is usually accurate to assume that little or no change in drinking behavior has taken place.

17. Game Playing

One might then ask why such clients would even bother to seek treatment. Almost always the reason is coercion or pressure from others. By getting counseling "help" the immediate pressure from others is reduced, and the "pressurers" are conned into believing that clients are being forthright with the counselor about their continued drinking. Thus, everyone is temporarily pleased: the counselor believes that such clients are making a sincere effort, and the pressurers believe that even though the clients still drink, they are getting help and quitting is only a matter of time. The game can actually go on for quite some time before someone catches on. Usually it's the pressurer, rather than the counselor, who finally draws the conclusion that the "help" is not working. The counselor is contacted, and is surprised (and embarrassed) to learn that he or she has been conned.

While accurate detection of the con game may prove quite difficult, suspicion can be aroused fairly early in treatment. For almost all alcoholics, giving up alcohol is painful, hard work. Thus, there is good reason for suspicion if clients report that they are doing quite well and are not experiencing any discomfort. (Most conners tend to overdo the descriptions about how well things are going.) Once the suspicion has been aroused, the counselor cannot wait indefinitely for the "truth." There is little purpose in continuing treatment until the suspicion has either been confirmed or put to rest. Since it would be a breach of trust to discuss the matter privately with the pressurers, the counselor is obliged to deal directly with the clients. Direct expression might negatively affect the counseling relationship, but in this case concern over that possibility is less relevant: there can hardly *be* a valid relationship if clients are engaging in deceptive behavior.

When the counselor is satisfied that clients appear to be doing *too* well, at the risk of losing them, direct confrontation should be used. If clients deny any deception and wish to continue in treatment, the author sometimes asks either for leave to speak with the pressurer (usually the spouse) or that the pressurer be invited to the next session. In most cases such a meeting never comes about, as clients wish to avoid the unpleasant experience of being confronted by both the counselor and the pressurer. If clients admit that they have not been candid, the counselor should respond without chastisement. A request for increased sincerity in the future will suffice. On the other hand, if the suspicion is not valid, a sincere apology is required as well as an explanation as to why the counselor was suspicious.

Outwitting behavior is an attempt to influence the content and direction of treatment. The game requires a bright client and an insecure, passive, or inexperienced counselor. The typical strategy is to distract the counselor from symptom management and to engage in an endless search to understand "why I drink." The unspoken message is: "I cannot stop drinking until I have gained sufficient insight into why I *do* drink." As in other manipulative games, outwitting behavior need not require conscious awareness; many clients play the game without realizing that it is an attempt to control. However, one thing all outwitters are aware of is their unwillingness to give up alcohol.

Some counselors fall easily into the trap, particularly those who have been trained to employ insight-oriented treatment and feel most comfortable with it. They follow such clients' leads into the realm of unconscious defense mechanisms, intrapsychic conflicts, and early childhood experiences, feeling rewarded by the occasional breakthroughs (major insights) and secure in the belief that *they* are controlling the direction of treatment. Such counselors often sincerely believe that when alcoholics understand why they drink, in all likelihood they will be able to stop. These counselors have accepted the rules of the game.

For a while all parties are satisfied, with the clients continuing to drink until they have "gained further insight," the counselor in hot pursuit of new leads that might help illuminate the underlying psychodynamics, and families pleased that the clients are finally doing something about their drinking. But satisfaction is likely to give way to frustration when the counselor realizes that although these clients have now gained sufficient insight to at least reduce their drinking, they continue to maintain the same level of alcohol consumption. The counselor's blunder is that instead of helping such clients to control their drinking behavior, he or she has unwittingly supplied them with an excuse — even a *justification* — for continued drinking: as clients continue to drink, they can now explain to themselves why they do it.

17. Game Playing

Whatever form of treatment a counselor employs, the primary consideration must be symptom management. Otherwise it is unlikely that treatment will have any long-range impact. If clients want to work on understanding the causes of their drinking, they should demonstrate good faith by also working on abstinence, as there is no evidence that insight, alone, leads to behavior change. And the course of treatment should be determined by the counselor (with an appreciation of clients' needs), *not* by clients. In general, clients who insist on insight first have little or no commitment to changing their drinking behavior.

Purposeful misinterpretation is most likely to occur when the counselor makes remarks or recommendations that are unclear, leaving clients with considerable latitude for interpretation. Misinterpretation becomes a game when clients do not ask for clarification, preferring to choose a possible meaning most in keeping with their needs. Thus, "You should make some attempt to do something about your alcohol intake," is sufficiently vague for game-playing clients to avoid asking, "What do you mean?" or "Do you have any ideas about how I should do it?" Instead, they might respond, "Yes, you're right," meaning that at some future date something as yet unspecified should be done but that there is no imperative to act now — which is the opposite of what the counselor had intended to convey. Thus, such clients continue drinking at their usual rate to the consternation of the counselor, who demands, "I thought you were going to take some action about your drinking." The "innocent" clients then reply, "Yes, I agreed to do something, but you didn't tell me what to do or when to do it."

When clients take advantage of the counselor's lack of clarity, should they be held accountable? No. The counselor must leave no opportunity for alternative interpretation when making a recommendation, interpretation, or significant remark, and should verify clients' understanding by asking them to respond to what has been said. (In fact, any significant statements should be recorded as close to verbatim as possible at the conclusion of a session.) If an important statement cannot be expressed clearly, it usually indicates that the counselor has not thought it through clearly, leaving a game-playing client to purposely misinterpret and very possibly confusing a sincere client. Therefore, if this game does occur, it is with the counselor's assistance.

Frequently changing the subject usually occurs during a struggle for control, with the counselor attempting to pursue certain issues he or she believes to be relevant and clients attempting to avoid those very topics and to introduce others. What is discussed indicates who is in control.

This game is often indicative of a larger struggle in which counselor and client can be viewed as "combatants," each trying to move in a different direction and avoiding giving up any ground. In this larger struggle, the counselor is fearful of losing control and thus losing face, and the client is fearful of being controlled and thus becoming overly dependent. Hence, if such clients attempt to change the subject, the rules of the game require that the counselor not permit it. The counselor is in a powerful position to compel clients to "stay in line" or else be judged as uncooperative, unwilling to face reality, undermining treatment, etc. This situation is hardly a healthy and therapeutic atmosphere, and in the overwhelming number of cases there is no reason for it to develop.

It should be anticipated when working with alcoholic clients that testing behavior is quite common. By frequently changing the subject, clients may very well be testing how much room they have to manoeuvre when "sensitive" issues are brought up: Will the counselor back away from or continue to pursue the sensitive issue? This sort of testing can easily set the stage for a power struggle. How the counselor responds will determine whether there is to be an escalation of the struggle (with the client being perceived as playing games at the counselor's expense), a capitulation by backing off (with the counselor feeling that control has been surrendered to the client), or, most appropriately, a disregarding of the issue of control (with the counselor recognizing the behavior as a form of testing, requiring neither an authoritarian nor a capitulating response).

The following examples may help to clarify this somewhat complex interaction between counselor and client: "I noticed that

17. Game Playing

you changed the subject and I'd like to know why you want to avoid it" (an authoritarian challenge to clients to "get back in line"); "I noticed that you changed the subject; all right, let's set it aside for the time being" (backing off); or "I noticed that you changed the subject" (a nonthreatening observation, neither challenging nor backing off). The third approach merely presents an accurate statement to which clients are obliged to respond; how they respond is up to them. The statement is sufficiently neutral to avoid a power struggle, and neither client nor counselor is placed in jeopardy. As is the case with so many other forms of gaming behavior, this one cannot flourish without the counselor's (presumably) unwitting assistance. A power struggle develops only if both parties engage in it.

Intellectual discourses, when initiated by clients, suggest a need to distract attention from themselves and to draw the counselor into an interesting but irrelevant discussion. Sometimes, particularly with very bright clients, the counselor may experience considerable ego involvement in such discourses as they provide a platform for "proving" that he or she is as smart as the client. If the counselor finds such discussions challenging or rewarding, chances are that these clients will take advantage of any opportunity to play this game. And once the discourses begin to occur on a regular basis, it will be increasingly difficult to refocus attention on basic treatment issues. The clients have, in effect, exploited a need of the counselor in order to render him or her impotent as a treater.

If it weren't for the fact that such clients are very much in need of counseling assistance, their behavior could be viewed as highly successful manipulation. Quite often, though, intellectually oriented clients are uncomfortable in experiencing or expressing emotions. They employ the defense mechanism of "intellectualization" to neutralize feeling and to cope with conscious emotion in a "thinking" manner. Thus, a potentially upsetting experience may, for example, remind such clients of a poem or a chapter in a book, which permits them to acknowledge and discuss the existence of certain feelings without experiencing them personally. Alcohol provides an outlet for these clients, temporarily lowering their defenses so that repressed emotion can be consciously and somewhat comfortably expressed. With such clients it is counter-therapeutic to engage in frequent intellectual interchanges, for this not only renders the counselor ineffective but also reinforces a pathological life adjustment.

Although the author considers intellectual discourses a game, in that the result is control or manipulation of the counselor, it is very much a desperate game. An integral part of treatment should be to minimize intellectual interaction (explaining to clients why this is necessary), and in the relative security of the counselor's office to work first on experiencing and then on expressing feelings. In the long run such clients are good candidates for group therapy, even if the group is not composed of individuals with alcohol problems, as the relatively secure environment of the group provides opportunities to test emotional expression and to receive feedback from peers. The increased ability to consciously experience emotion and to express it appropriately removes one of the major roles of alcohol in such clients' lives, and thus the probability of more successful control of alcohol consumption is enhanced.

Unreasonable demands by clients continue only with the counselor's cooperation and encouragement. The role of "rescuer," as viewed by Steiner (1969), consists of an inappropriate willingness on the part of the counselor to respond to unreasonable client demands. To prevent this situation from developing, the counselor must respond decisively at the first occurrence.

Dependent clients and those who have a history of crises (arrests, marital discord, dismissals from jobs, financial debts, etc.) are the most likely to make unreasonable demands. The combination of a concerned, sympathetic counselor and a crisis-oriented client sets the stage for the counselor to respond inappropriately to the immediate needs of the client. Although superficially it might appear that the counselor is acting with compassion and in the best interests of such clients, exactly the opposite is true. The clients are learning to expect the counselor to intervene on their behalf and to bail them out of crisis situations. Furthermore, in the long run, they come to view such interventions as the responsibility of the counselor, and no longer concern themselves with solving their own difficulties. By continually giving clients the benefit of the doubt, the counselor is unwittingly reinforcing their dependence. When the counselor finally recognizes that clients are taking unfair advantage, it is often too late for corrective action. Such clients have, with the cooperation of the counselor, manipulated the situation to a point where it probably cannot be brought under control without severe damage to the therapeutic relationship, as the clients' expectations of treatment resulted directly from the counselor's willingness to be manipulated.

Many alcoholic clients tend to be overly dependent and, due to their alcoholism, are directly responsible for many of the crises in their lives. It is almost axiomatic that a major goal of treatment should be increased self-reliance: learning either to avoid or to cope with crisis situations. Early in treatment many such clients may attempt to test the counselor by making an unreasonable demand (e.g. to contact an employer and suggest that the client is improving; to contact the spouse who may be threatening to leave and request that the decision be postponed; to see the client after usual office hours because the client "just can't make it" before then). Although many counselors find it difficult to say no when all that is requested is a brief telephone call or a temporary rearrangement of their schedules, more often than not "no" is the best answer. The counselor should make it clear that such a request *might* be appropriate at some later date in treatment, but until the counselor knows the client much better, the request cannot be met. This does *not* mean that a neutral note or telephone call merely stating that a client has sought treatment is out of order. That is a legitimate request which the counselor can honor without compromise. There may even be an occasion where the counselor's intervention is appropriate, but clients must be informed that this is an exception to the rule and that they should not anticipate further interventions.

After making an unreasonable demand that is legitimately rejected by the counselor, some clients will drop out of treatment and not be heard from again. This clearly suggests that their agenda was to use the counselor as an intervenor on their behalf, not to seek active treatment for their alcoholism. There is no reason whatsoever for the counselor to feel that he or she has let such clients down.

The author has observed that those clients whose counselors actively respond to unreasonable demands tend to have more frequent and intense crises than those whose counselors are less willing to cooperate. Perhaps if clients know that they will be "bailed out," they are more likely to precipitate crises.

Flattery, praise, and gifts may in certain restricted circumstances be appropriate, but in general they are not. It is not out of order for clients to remark that an article of clothing worn by the counselor is attractive, or to express praise for the counselor's wisdom in having made a recommendation that proved to be beneficial, or to send a card or other small token of appreciation at the successful *termination* of treatment. However, such attentions become a game when they begin to occur frequently. In that case, what appear to be thoughtful gestures may in fact be part of clients' hidden agendas, and usually have one of two meanings.

The first possibility is that certain clients may harbor resentment and hostility towards the counselor. Unable to consciously accept their feelings, they repress them and through reaction-formation behave in an overly positive manner towards the counselor. This game is unlikely to be overtly manipulative, but rather is dictated by clients' unconscious defenses and motives. (Working with such clients is discussed in Section 8: "Clients' Hostility towards the Counselor.")

The other major possibility is almost always a serious game as it is a move to control or manipulate the counselor's feelings. In this case, clients are attempting to win acceptance and to increase their chances of being liked by the counselor. The counselor who regularly tolerates such behavior may be in jeopardy of becoming "in debt" to such clients, which makes objective judgment more difficult and quite possibly reduces the counselor's effectiveness. Therefore, as well as attempting to win acceptance, such clients may succeed in throwing the counselor "off balance" through subtle and probably unwitting manipulation of the therapeutic relationship. It is certainly more difficult to be firm and constructively critical of someone who consistently offers flattery and praise. Thus, *if* the behavior has been accepted by the counselor, the clients' overriding concern to be liked has caused detrimental side effects.

This strategy is one that such clients probably employ frequently in everyday life: attack with praise and flattery to disarm others, thereby increasing the chances of being liked and reducing the chances of rejection or hostility. It is a strategy based on deep feelings of insecurity and low self-esteem. These individuals, feeling subordinate to others, believe they must *earn* acceptance and approval, for they strongly doubt that they will be liked on their own merits. If the strategy works, such individuals have manipulated feelings out of subordination rather than dominance. But it can only work if others are susceptible to praise and flattery — and the "debt" owed for continuing praise is continuing positive expression towards the flatterer. *That* could be a potentially serious bind for the responsive counselor.

Flattery and praise need not be disruptive if the counselor simply ignores the behavior or, of more benefit to clients, works with them to strengthen feelings of self-esteem. A counselor who understands the dynamics of flattery and praise is in a position to provide such clients with the experience of being accepted and liked without having to resort to the typical strategy. These clients have much to profit from group therapy as well, because the strategy will undoubtedly be picked up by the other group members, who probably will find it unacceptable, thus requiring clients to risk standing on their own merits.

18

Verbally Threatening Behavior when Sober

This occurs so infrequently in alcoholism counseling that the author is aware of only a few cases. They fall into two categories: either the client was schizophrenic or the counselor made a gross error in judgment.

Schizophrenic clients who also have an alcohol problem should be referred to a pyschiatrist who has access to hospital admission, should that become necessary. While the overwhelming majority of schizophrenics, alcoholic or not, present no real danger, occasionally a paranoid schizophrenic whose auditory hallucinations urge violent behavior or who is experiencing a delusion that, for example, the counselor is an "agent of the devil" can present a very serious threat. Although it is improbable that any given counselor will encounter even a single such case in his or her career, the slight possibility of occurrence requires some guidelines.

A counselor must *never* dispute the delusions of a schizophrenic by insisting or even suggesting that what the client believes to be reality is untrue. The delusions must be accepted in a neutral manner or with sympathetic support and understanding. Disagreement, particularly when a schizophrenic is behaving in a threatening manner, only serves to convince the client that the counselor is lying and therefore must be an enemy. If the client makes bizarre statements, the counselor should ask in an interested manner, "Please tell me more about that." If the schizophrenic believes that the counselor is genuinely interested and sympathetic, the immediate threat will probably be reduced. Assuming the client is willing to leave without incident, the counselor should say that arrangements will be made for the client to see an "understanding doctor." (The word "psychiatrist" should be avoided.) The client should then be asked to wait in the lobby while the counselor telephones the nearest hospital with a psychiatric service. The counselor might wish to explain the situation to the on-call psychiatrist, who can suggest the most appropriate course of action.

Threatening behavior in sober *nonpsychotics* may be in reaction to an ill-considered recommendation by the counselor. For example, advising a client to "have it out" with his spouse may lead to a furious debate, with the wife packing her bags and leaving. The client is likely to hold the counselor responsible and, in some instances, may threaten the counselor. In most cases such a threat is not carried out *unless* the counselor compounds his or her judgmental error by insisting that the outcome was the client's fault. This is not the time to assess blame.

The counselor can best reduce the immediate threat by acknowledging responsibility: "I hadn't anticipated that your wife would take such drastic action." Provided the counselor is not overwhelmed with fear, attention should be directed towards appreciating the client's anger and suggesting a remedy: "Let's see what can be done to rectify the situation." If the counselor is too frightened to respond constructively, the client should be told how frightening his behavior is, and that if he is unwilling to calm down the counselor will have to get help. Responding angrily to a client's threats should definitely be avoided as it is likely to stimulate further aggression.

If such clients do calm down at least to a point where constructive discussion is possible, then it would seem appropriate to continue treatment after offering them the opportunity to see someone else. If clients leave, still angry, chances are that they will not return or be willing to accept further treatment. Although such an outcome would be unfortunate, at least the counselor should have learned a lesson about giving direct advice without having sufficient information.

19
Suicidal Tendency

Milt's review (1967) of the literature indicates that approximately 30% of all those who attempt suicide are alcoholics. This is in keeping with the author's observations while directing a crisis intervention unit in a large Toronto hospital: alcoholics represent the largest identifiable group of suicide attempters. One of the general effects of alcohol is the intensification of already existing depression in the individual, and therefore those who attempt suicide frequently do so after they have been drinking. Considering the frequency with which depression is encountered in alcoholics (Roebuck and Kessler, 1972), the counselor should anticipate that *some* alcoholic clients may have suicidal tendencies.

Variables to Consider
1. assessing suicidal risk
2. appropriate courses of action to prevent suicide attempt
3. counseling after suicide attempt

Although over the past two decades several scales of criteria for potential suicide risk have been developed, none has proved effective. While it is accurate to view almost all suicide attempters as depressed, the majority of depressed individuals are not suicidal. But it is better for the counselor to err on the side of caution rather than to assume that depressed clients present no suicidal risk.

Certain behaviors suggest the *possibility* of increased risk. The following indicators should always be taken seriously:

1. History of previous suicidal behavior, especially while under the influence of alcohol. This is the most reliable indicator of possible future attempts, and such clients *must* agree to total abstinence during treatment.

2. References to feelings of futility such as "I don't care whether I live or die," or "Life isn't worth living." Such statements must be viewed seriously as almost all suicide attempters "tip their hands" prior to the attempt. (Many nonsuicidal individuals have days when they feel like this. Repetition is the key factor.)

3. Preoccupation with dying and direct references such as "I've thought about death a lot lately," or "Sometimes I feel that I would like to kill myself."

4. Reports of increased depression when drinking.

5. Recent crisis or loss such as severe marital conflict, the spouse leaving home, job loss, death of a loved one, or learning of a serious illness. It should be kept in mind that most suicide attempts are precipitated by crisis or loss.

6. Continual expressions of hopelessness, of feeling trapped, of "going nowhere." Such clients report that from their perspective an unhappy life situation has no possibility of positive resolution, or that they view their lives as meaningless and unrewarding.

7. Dramatic mood swings from depression to feeling "at peace" or "okay" without any external events to account for the mood changes. In some clients this may suggest that the conflict over death has been resolved in favor of killing themselves. While a suicide attempt is usually impulsive, in response to a sudden increase in stress, a serious plan to kill oneself is often preceded by feeling of well-being, as the pressure of decision-making has been removed.

8. Improvement in severely depressed clients. Despite their desire to commit suicide, most severely depressed individuals do not have the energy to do it; for them, just getting up in the morning is a debilitating experience. As the severity of the depressive episode begins to lift, however, such individuals become more capable of action. Severely depressed clients should be hospitalized.

(Jacobs, 1975)

If two or more of the above indicators are present, or if any one appears particularly intense, psychiatric consultation is advisable. Whether or not the psychiatrist decides upon hospitalization, the consultation will provide the counselor with expert assessment and recommended approaches, as well as a contact if the situation worsens in the future.

Clients who appear to be seriously suicidal should be directed immediately to the emergency department of the nearest hospital and, when possible, should be accompanied by the counselor. The counselor can provide the attending physician with information that will help in making a comprehensive assessment, and the counselor's presence may also be reassuring to clients.

A suicidal gesture (where the individual expects to be "saved") should be treated as seriously as the real thing. It is a cry for help, and if help is not forthcoming such individuals just might take their lives. The problem for the counselor is rarely one of unconcern but rather of overreaction. The author knows of no other client behavior (with the exception of a threat of direct assault) that so profoundly affects the counselor. Self-recrimination, guilt, and a preoccupation with the question "Where did I go wrong?" are typical responses.

It must be kept in mind that the counselor's role is not one of "savior" or "rescuer." Even though the counselor may have been cognizant of all the indicators mentioned above, the behavior of alcoholics can change so dramatically under the influence of alcohol — and invariably in ways that the counselor has not witnessed — that sometimes suicidal behavior cannot be predicted. The counselor must set aside self-recrimination and concentrate on the immediate needs of the client.

Even if suicidal clients have been rushed to an emergency department, unless there are physical complications they are often discharged and returned to the counselor. A calm, empathetic, reassuring approach is recommended. The counselor should try to understand the conditions that precipitated the suicidal behavior and to encourage such clients by saying that those precipitating problems will be worked on with an attempt (but not a promise) to find solutions. In addition, and without condemnation, the counselor should initiate discussion of the clients' behavior and feelings while drinking. It is appropriate to stress to suicidal clients that alcohol only tends to exacerbate depression, and to ask them to genuinely reaffirm the contract not to use it while in treatment.

20

Age, Sex, and Professional Status of the Counselor

Variables to Consider
1. mature clients and young counselors
2. defensive, resistant clients
3. clients and counselors of opposite sex
4. handling provocative, seductive behavior
5. clients' negative perception of counselor's professional status
6. counselor's negative perception of own professional status

A significant age difference between counselor and client is quite common in alcoholism treatment, as recent graduates, particularly social workers, often begin their careers in community agencies where they are required to work with clients of all ages. While there is abundant research to support the notion that the experience of the counselor correlates positively with treatment outcome, the same cannot be said of age *per se*. Through clinical observation of young but enthusiastic counselors, Strupp (1971) suggests that in many instances they are more effective than certain of their more experienced colleagues. This might be particularly true in alcoholism counseling. Given the high failure rate in alcoholism treatment, older and more experienced counselors may tend to be less optimistic and somewhat "jaded" in their expectations of treatment. Younger and less experienced counselors, however, having encountered fewer failures, are more likely to create a positive outcome expectancy for alcoholic clients. This assumes, of course, that older clients are not negatively affected by the age of the assigned counselor.

From clients' perspectives, age is generally not a major factor because it is overridden by the perceived status of the counselor. Nevertheless, if clients raise the issue, it can be dealt with in a forthright manner.

It is not unusual for clients several years older than their youthful counselors to react initially with surprise. (The average age of alcoholic clients in outpatient treatment is 40 to 45 years.) It is likely that such clients would have expected the counselor, as is probably the case with their doctor, to be their peer in age. Quite understandably, clients in their mid-40s may have reservations about accepting counseling from someone young enough to be a son or daughter.

The key to resolving the problem is a nondefensive attitude on the part of the counselor. It is inappropriate for the counselor to place himself or herself on trial. Presenting one's credentials or reassuring clients that expert supervision is being provided is usually all that is required. If clients remain unconvinced, the counselor might suggest, "Let's try it for a few sessions and reassess your feelings after we've gotten to know each other." Once the clients have had the opportunity to determine that the counselor *is* professionally competent, the subject of age is usually laid to rest.

Very strong objections are raised most commonly by clients who are defensive and resistant to treatment. Such clients are usually attempting to find reasons to support their unwillingness to pursue counseling. Thus the rationalization "He can't help me; he's just a kid" is unlikely to be modified even after the counselor's competence has been amply demonstrated, and age may well be used as justification to discontinue counseling. In this case, transfer to an older counselor should be suggested. However, clients seeking reasons to drop out will probably have little difficulty finding other attributes of the new counselor that are unacceptable.

Given the increasing numbers of women entering the helping professions during the past two decades, it is now common for male clients to be assigned to female counselors. Although this usually presents few problems, there are some instances that deserve consideration. Many male alcoholics have a history of difficulty in relating to members of the opposite sex. While they may not openly express anxieties at being assigned to a female counselor, it is advisable for her to be aware that some male clients might feel uncomfortable initially. Usually any anxieties such clients might feel are laid to rest after a few contacts, as sufficient opportunities have been provided for clients to recognize that their female counselor is competent and professional in manner. Indeed, a few clinicians have remarked that a female counselor can be more effective than a male, due to the frequently reported dependency needs in male alcoholics. (The author finds this statement both ill-conceived and chauvinistic as it suggests that the appropriate role for female counselors is a motherly one.)

Some male clients, usually those with serious sexual adjustment problems, may express an unwillingness to continue working with a female counselor after the first interview. They may simply ask whether it is possible to see a male counselor, without explaining why. Vigorously pursuing reasons for the request at this very early stage is not advised as it will probably prove unnecessarily embarrassing to these clients. But immediate transfer to a male counselor without further ado may also be ill-advised. Asking the clients to agree to attend a few more sessions is in order, for in the long run, contact with an unthreatening and accepting female counselor may be most beneficial to clients who have difficulties relating to women. After some degree of comfort has been reached, the possibilities for the role playing of typically upsetting encounters with women and the chances of reaching successful resolutions are obviously much greater — and more real — with a female rather than a male counselor. Furthermore, positive contact with a woman *may* help male clients to relate more successfully to other women. However, if such clients are either adamant in their request or it appears that they may drop out of treatment if forced to continue with the female counselor, a transfer to a male is probably in their *short-term* best interests.

Women counselors employed in social agencies that serve economically disadvantaged groups should be alerted to the particular dissonance created for male clients when working with a counselor of the opposite sex. There is abundant literature pertaining to the typically subordinate role of women and the entrenched attitude of men towards maintaining this role in many lower-income groups. Therefore, it may take some time for lower-income males to feel comfortable with a female counselor, and how she responds to him is important. She must take care not to permit her own values to impinge upon the treatment relationship, which already has one major obstacle to overcome. Provided the female counselor can accept the difference in values between herself and her male client, any dissonance is usually reduced or eliminated once treatment focuses on symptom management and "here and now" problems. Usually such clients then begin to perceive the counselor less in terms of her sex and status, and more as a concerned, reality-oriented problem solver who works with them in attempting to find solutions.

Occasionally, male clients may attempt to manipulate the treatment situation, usually during the early phase, by referring directly to the female counselor's sex, by making provocative statements, or by acting in a seductive manner. The counselor is advised to view such behavior as a probable attempt by such clients to avoid dealing with their own problems and/or to engage the counselor in a powerful struggle. There are two reasonable approaches. The counselor may choose not to react at all, except for a neutral and indifferently presented statement like "Let's concern ourselves with other matters." (Neutral responses often extinguish manipulative behavior.) Or, if sexual references or seductive behavior continue, an alternative approach is to confront clients directly. The counselor should acknowledge without recrimination her awareness of the client's behavior, pointing out that it distracts him from his reasons for being in treatment — "So let's get back on track." Although some may be disinclined to contend with such behavior directly, in the long run it is far better to dispose of it than to permit it to persist, as it is invariably counter-productive. Confrontation in this situation is honest and constructive, it is the counselor who sets the controls and places limits on the interactions between client and counselor. In addition, direct confrontation is contrary to the expectations of the client, who most likely intended his behavior to elicit discomfort, thereby granting him a temporary "edge" in his power struggle with her. Dealing openly with such inappropriate behavior will more likely reduce the chances of a power struggle developing, as the female counselor has expressed an awareness of the behavior and an unwillingness to play the game without rebuking the client.

The same approach is recommended for a male counselor in contending with provocative statements or seductive behavior by female clients. As is the case with male clients, some female clients with serious sexual adjustment problems or who have had difficulty in relating to men may experience temporary discomfort when working with a male counselor. For the same reasons noted above, it may prove beneficial for a female client to attempt to continue with her assigned male counselor, and referral to a female counselor should only be considered if such clients are adamant or wish to discontinue treatment.

With the exception of one fairly well-researched instance, problems relating to the negatively perceived professional status of the counselor originate more often in the counselor than in clients. The one instance where the counselor's professional status is reported to be somewhat relevant is with clients from lower socioeconomic groups. Mayer and Myerson (1971), among others, report that many lower-income alcoholics prefer to be treated by physicians; they tend to view their problem as medical, and therefore worthy of attention by a "doctor" who dispenses medicine. In reality, however, the majority of lower-income clients are not counseled by MDs. And although lower social status *per se* is often incorrectly reported as an indicator of poor prognosis for alcoholics, counselors — regardless of degree — can have a significant impact. (Working with lower-income alcoholic clients is discussed in Section 21: "Social Class and Culture.")

At the other end of the continuum, upper-status and well-educated clients are most likely to seek treatment from private psychiatrists, which suggests that they view their alcoholism as a psychological problem worthy of treatment only by the professional perceived to be most qualified in that field. (Recall, however, the negative views held by many psychiatrists towards alcoholics reported in Section 4: "Motivation.")

In an MD-oriented society, where tremendous status is granted to physicians, other helping professionals often experience feelings of inferiority. Although there is little evidence that physicians are more effective in counseling alcoholic clients, the author has observed what can only be described as an apologetic attitude on the part of some nonmedical counselors regarding their "lower" qualifications. Nonsense! The mystique that some patients ascribe to physicians *may* give them a temporary edge, but that is usually all. Nonmedical workers are best advised to disregard comparisons of qualifications and effectiveness between themselves and medical personnel. Confidence in one's ability (as opposed to lack of confidence or over-confidence) is a decided asset in counseling alcoholic clients, no matter what degree or diploma the counselor holds. Indeed, clients have every reason to assume the counselor is qualified by the very fact that he or she is practising. The subtle but powerful disruptive influence of this issue on treatment is *less* related to any negative perception on the part of clients than to negative self-perception by the counselor, which is often communicated unintentionally to clients. In the author's experience, effective alcoholism counselors run the gamut from community college graduates to MDs, but one factor they seem to have in common is their belief that they can be helpful. If there are other factors, they would more likely be related to personality traits than to the "pecking-order" status of the diploma or degree, a point that has been well demonstrated by Truax and Carkhuff (1967), among others.

21

Social Class and Culture

Hollingshead's and Redlich's landmark study (1958) clearly indicated that social class markedly affects both psychiatric diagnosis and type of treatment received. The author's observations in a variety of settings suggest that this is particularly true in the field of alcoholism. The traditional label of poor prognosis, "alcoholism," is most often attached to lower-status clients. Higher-status clients with similar symptoms usually receive the more benign and prognostically favorable diagnosis of "anxiety reaction" or "depression," with "alcohol abuse" (if the term is used at all) being relegated to secondary diagnosis.

Even when the diagnosis of "alcoholism" is applied to individuals of higher social status, there are clear differences in the types of treatment such clients receive and in who provides it (Schmidt et al., 1968; Redlich and Kellert, 1978). Redlich and Kellert, for example, have found that lower-status alcoholics in public, state hospitals virtually *never* have a psychiatrist as a counselor or even see one at any stage in treatment. Upper-status alcoholics in private facilities, on the other hand, almost *always* have a psychiatrist as their primary counselor.

It might be tempting to assume that because of the similarities in values between upper-status alcoholics and their counselors, such clients would be less likely to drop out of treatment than their lower-status counterparts (Strupp, 1971; Baekeland et al., 1975; and Larkin, 1974), and that, due to their possibly greater persistence in treatment, higher-status clients would also be more likely to recover from alcoholism (Baekeland et al., 1975).

However, despite the research presented by the above authors to support their positions, neither assumption is clearly valid. As many, if not more, studies on alcoholism have found

107

social status to be *unrelated* to drop-out from treatment (e.g. Gerard and Saenger, 1966; Schmidt et al., 1968; Madden, 1976; Bowen and Twemlow, 1978; Gerther et al., 1973; Krasnoff, 1976), and *unrelated* to treatment outcome (e.g. Gerard and Saenger, 1966; Armor et al., 1976; Gillies et al., 1974; Lowe and Thomas, 1976; Madden, 1976; Vallance, 1965; van Dijk and van Dijk-Koffeman, 1973).

The relationship between social status and alcoholism treatment is a complex matter. The apparently contradictory research findings may stem from the myriad personality and treatment characteristics that have yet to be clearly defined. However, given the large number of alcoholism studies that report no relationship between social class and treatment success, the common belief in the greater intractability of lower-class alcoholics must be viewed at least in part as folklore and prejudice.

Variables to Consider
1. counselor's biases regarding economically disadvantaged clients
2. drinking behavior and social class
3. low self-esteem among lower-status clients
4. counseling approaches
5. cultural differences between client and counselor

In the course of training numerous counselors in community agencies, the author has invariably asked, "Have any of you had any specific academic training that would prepare you to work with the economically disadvantaged?" The overwhelming response is "No," regardless of the type of academic degree program at either the graduate or undergraduate level. Furthermore, very few agencies provide on-the-job training. Hence, counselors have little option but to learn to work with lower-status clients on a trial and error basis.

There is abundant evidence that treatment staff are more comfortable with clients whose backgrounds are similar to their own (Strupp, 1971). Middle and upper-middle-class counselors live in a very different world from their lower-class clients: they are more future and success-oriented, depend more on abstract thinking, utilize complex verbal behavior as the primary means of communication (and are considerably more effective at it); they are less dependent on immediate gratification, placing greater emphasis on education and an awareness of the environment, are more restrictive in the direct expression of intense emotion, place a higher value on financial self-reliance, and relate to their spouses in a more egalitarian manner (Wrightsman, 1972; and Schmidt et al., 1968). Finally, while Riessman (1964) notes that middle-class individuals have their share of crises, the poor live constantly in a state of crisis.

The difficulties middle and upper-class counselors experience in understanding the values of lower-income individuals, their lifestyles, and their lesser capacity for verbal communication can lead to several biases. Schmidt et al. (1968) note that lower-class alcoholic clients are frequently given low ratings in motivation and insight, despite their finding that lower-class clients persist in therapy just as long as clients from other social classes. They further note that, in contrast to their counterparts from other social classes, "Talking therapy runs contrary to the expectations of many lower-class patients" (p. 88), an observation that often leads counselors to the erroneous conclusion that lower-class alcoholics are less cooperative, less motivated, and less capable of understanding treatment recommendations. It is common to view lower-class clients as having poor prognoses, and therefore many counselors are less than enthusiastic about treating them. It is the author's opinion that these biases can be overcome only through experience, through learning not to impose one's own value system on clients, and through developing treatment strategies that respect the differences between counselor and lower-class clients.

Before choosing appropriate treatment approaches, it is necessary to be aware of the differences in typical drinking patterns between lower-class individuals and those from other social classes. Although the percentage of heavy drinkers among lower-class men and women is as high or higher at all age levels than that for other social classes, there is *also* a higher percentage of abstainers among lower-class individuals (Cahalan et al., 1969). As Schmidt et al. (1968) report, members of the lower classes tend to drink at an earlier age, and symptoms of alcoholism usually appear earlier; their alcohol excesses are more extreme, with "sprees" more often resulting in arrest for gross public intoxication; there is greater tolerance for excessive drinking; their drinking patterns tend to be less regular and more disruptive; and finally, lower-class individuals are more likely to seek or to be pushed into treatment at a relatively young age.

Given the already existing biases against lower-class alcoholics, their behavioral excesses when intoxicated would appear only to strengthen most counselors' lack of enthusiasm about treating them. In general they are not "polite drinkers"; unlike the majority of middle and upper-class alcoholics, who tend to be "better behaved" when drunk, lower-class alcoholics engage more frequently in seriously disruptive behaviors, with a greater probability of extreme consequences. For this very reason, they desperately need assistance.

To meet lower-class alcoholic clients on their own ground requires that the counselor appreciate such clients' expectations. Most lower-class clients anticipate a medically oriented approach — not that the counselor must necessarily be a physician, but that treatment is expected to follow a medical model. Riessman et al. (1964) and Mayer and Myerson (1971) have observed that lower-class clients view as an "illness" what most members of other social classes consider a psychological problem. The "medical approach" involves direct advice, immediate support and encouragement, and an orientation towards symptom management and solutions, *not* towards psychodynamics and insight. Thus, wherever possible, collaboration with a physician who will perform a routine physical examination and prescribe appropriate medication is most desirable. This helps to fulfill clients' expectations of being treated for an illness. Unlike the approach with clients from other socioeconomic backgrounds where a few sessions "to get to know each other" are advisable, with lower-class clients intervention and advice should take place in the initial session. If this does not occur, Riessman et al. (1964) suggest there is a high probability that such clients will not return.

While advice should correspond to the specific needs of each client, there are some recommendations that can safely be offered to most lower-class alcoholics in the first session: attempt to cut down alcohol consumption; avoid visiting the hotel or pub where you usually drink; remove all alcohol from the house; eat regular, balanced, and nutritional meals (in the author's experience, the vast majority of lower-income alcoholics suffer from very poor dietary habits). In addition, clients should be given clear and simple-to-read pamphlets about alcoholism* and a physical examination should be made as soon as possible. Since many lower-income clients do not have a regular physician, the counselor should have available the name of a physician or health clinic and should even make the appointment with the physician before such clients leave. This demonstrates that the counselor is an action-oriented individual willing to "take charge" of the situation — which is usually reassuring to economically disadvantaged clients, many of whom suffer from feelings of helplessness.

Realistic support can also be offered in the initial session. As well as reassuring clients that their alcohol problems are treatable (with hard work), the counselor can give early attention to the numerous and very real problems that lower-class clients usually present. Employment problems, housing and financial difficulties, legal concerns, and problems with children and spouse are just a few of the most frequently heard complaints. Although realistically some problems just cannot be solved, if the counselor can assure such clients that their problems will be explored and attempts will be made to find solutions, they will be able to feel that someone who knows a lot more about the "system" than they do will try to intervene. Any person who routinely works with the economically disadvantaged is advised to keep a file of contacts in key agencies such as welfare, public housing, government-sponsored employment, training and education services, Children's Aid Society, legal aid, public health services, day-care centres, etc. Particularly in the early phases of treatment, the author has frequently played the role of advocate by cutting through bureaucratic red tape, because contending with the

---

*Suitable materials can be obtained from: Information Centre, Addiction Research Foundation, 33 Russell Street, Toronto, Ontario, Canada M5S 2S1

alcohol problems of lower-class clients cannot be separated from contending with social, economic, and family problems. If such clients perceive the counselor as willing to "work" for them, quite likely they will make a greater effort to carry out treatment recommendations.

Later sessions should maintain the same basic approach: an emphasis on immediate problems, a concrete orientation towards symptom management, training to improve daily living skills, active intervention (including occasional mediation with other agencies), directiveness where appropriate, and a good deal of support and praise.

There are a few other useful guidelines for working with lower-class alcoholics. Sessions need not take the traditional full hour; although an hour may be set aside, less time may actually be needed for the content of any given session. In fact, because many lower-class clients are painfully aware of their limitations in the face of the counselor's verbal skills, they may experience discomfort and irritation in talking sessions that last as long as an hour. If only 20 or 30 minutes are required for a session, the counselor should not feel that the client is being "cheated" or that other topics must be found to fill up the hour. Professional jargon should be avoided completely, as it is unlikely to be comprehended by economically disadvantaged clients, who, in order to save embarrassment, probably will not ask for clarification. A common problem, particularly for lower-income women, is fearfulness at leaving their own familiar surroundings and having to take public transportation to the counselor's office. Support, tolerance, and understanding should be forthcoming. It may even be necessary for the counselor to write out detailed directions as to how to get to the office and what means of public transportation to use. The cost of transportation should be discussed, as there are agencies (e.g. welfare) that can provide the necessary funds for office visits.

While the counselor can expect middle-class clients to do much of the talking during sessions and frequently to generate topics for discussion, this is not the case with many lower-income individuals. Since lower-class clients are likely to have experienced several unfavorable events between weekly sessions, they may not know where to begin, and must rely on the counselor to initiate and maintain the flow of discussion. One early goal for the counselor is to help clients determine the priority of subjects to be discussed, i.e. what requires immediate attention or intervention and what can be postponed. Although clients' alcoholism remains a high-priority subject, at times it may have to take second place to an immediate crisis.

Lower-class clients are often involved with more than one community or government agency. It is desirable, with clients' permission, to have contact with the other agencies in order to ensure that two or more counselors are not working at cross-purposes when they could be collaborating on a more comprehensive program.

If the counselor hopes to have any lasting impact on the alcohol problems of lower-class clients, certain realities must be taken into account. The feelings of low self-esteem so commonly encountered in alcoholics are intensely magnified in economically disadvantaged alcoholics. Apart from the typical factors contributing to low self-esteem, such as poor relationships with others, dependency, inability to control alcohol consumption, etc., lower-class alcoholics' feelings of self-worth are dramatically impaired by their position at the bottom of the social and economic scale. The middle-class values of education, a good job, financial security, and feeling that one is contributing to society have been denied to members of the lower classes, and consequently they are ill-prepared to function in a society that lauds such values. The mass media, particularly television, only serve to remind lower-class individuals of how far the "good life" is from their seemingly inescapable poverty. The feelings of hopelessness and helplessness are often coped with by a veneer of apathy, which counselors too often interpret as lack of motivation. The more valid, angry feelings of lower-class individuals are often exhibited while intoxicated, clearly suggesting that what appears to be apathy is only a superficial defense. As well as being one of the few sources of pleasure available to members of the lower classes, alcohol is a vehicle through which pent-up frustration and anger can be released. This, at least in part, accounts for Schmidt's observation of the behavioral excesses of the lower classes while under the influence of alcohol.

More often than not, lower-income male alcoholics are coerced into treatment by legal authorities or spouses because their behavior while drinking is legally and socially unacceptable. Similarly, lower-status female alcoholics, who may have been abandoned by their spouses or may never have been married, common-law or otherwise, are also frequently coerced by community agencies that "hold the purse strings" and/or are directly involved with the well-being of their children. However, apart from the stipulation that such individuals obtain assistance for their "illness," there are few if any reasons for lower-class alcoholics to abstain. The challenge for the counselor is not only to deal directly with the symptom, but to encourage feelings of self-worth by providing personal support and praise, and by initiating action to help such clients obtain their "share of the pie" through skill upgrading, educational programs, and specialized training programs. In addition, immediate opportunities to engage in rewarding activities or make desired purchases can be made available through the rebudgeting of income, as abstinence frees money that was previously spent on alcohol.

Realistically, however, the inertia or "resistance to change" is difficult to overcome, and the constant interruptions of immediate problems and crises may impede progress. Patience is an absolute necessity when working with lower-class alcoholics, for their whole lives have prepared them to feel doomed to failure. From the beginning of treatment, the counselor must be intensely responsive to mini-successes — must even search for something positive in what appears to be a failure. For example, an alcoholic who is advised to abstain but who then proceeds to drink six days out of seven may not objectively appear to be doing well *unless* the counselor places great significance on the single day of abstinence. In the early stages of treatment, counselors should provide simple homework assignments that have a built-in high probability of success, e.g. assigning clients who feel unable to cope with their messy homes the task of washing the dishes every day. When that has been mastered, a more complicated assignment can be given, such as keeping the rest of the kitchen in order.

Success breeds success; with the increasing mastery of tasks that previously seemed impossible, the willingness of such clients to try new things will be enhanced, and so will their self-esteem.

Abstinence assignments should parallel the step-by-step mastering of other success-oriented tasks. The counselor might suggest, for example, that clients increase the number of days between drinks or decrease the amount of alcohol intake at any given time. There will be setbacks, and they should be anticipated. The counselor should play down failure, letting clients know that he or she believes they can get back on track. It may seem a long road from trying to wash dishes and drinking almost daily to successfully completing a skills training program and achieving abstinence. But in many instances lower-class alcoholics *can* reorient themselves from failure to the belief that success is possible, *provided* the counselor does not adhere to the unwarranted middle-class belief that the poor are unmotivated and unable to help themselves.

While there is a growing awareness today of the different forms alcoholism may take, depending upon cultural and ethnic factors, it is not within the scope of this book to examine the wide range of cultural groups that a counselor might encounter. There are, however, a few general guidelines that might prove helpful:

1. The greater the cultural disparity between counselor and client, the less the likelihood of positive treatment outcome.
2. Treatment should rarely be undertaken if there is a significant language barrier, and *never* if the presence of an interpreter is required.
3. A file should be kept of counselors who either have had considerable experience with or are members of cultural groups with a sizable representation in the community.
4. Although academic training can be helpful in overcoming cultural barriers, it is not a substitute for the experience of working with other counselors who are more familiar with the culture of a particular client. Instead of merely referring such clients, the counselor should take advantage of this opportunity to broaden his or her effectiveness.

5. If a counselor is alone in providing service to members of other ethnic and cultural groups, it is essential that his or her values not be imposed on clients. Discussions with family members and sometimes the clergy can help the counselor to understand the parameters for acceptable and unacceptable drinking behaviors within the particular culture.

22

Wife's* Vested Interest in Client's Alcoholism

The wife of an alcoholic lives in a precarious situation, what with her husband's possibly unpredictable, abusive, or even violent behavior when drinking, her feelings of embarrassment, her vacillation between love and anger, and her sense of being trapped in a hopeless existence. Over and over again she has experienced the severe disappointment of her husband returning to alcohol after declarations to quit, and she tries to shield herself from further disappointment by accepting the reality that his promises hold no substance.

For many wives, the only reasonable recourse is separation or divorce, and these options are selected at a significantly higher rate than among the general population. However, although brief separations are common, most wives of alcoholics do remain with their husbands, and this often requires rationalization, self-deception, and the continuous need to justify their perseverance to concerned relatives. Some common coping strategies are: "Where could I go?" "How could I provide for myself and the children?" "He's sick and can't help it," "I just know that someday he'll quit," "When he's not drinking we get along fine," "He needs me," "At least he's a good provider," "I'll try to go about my life in spite of him," and "I'll just have to carry the burden as best as I can." If the spouses of alcoholics have anything in common it is

---

*Little or no research is available on the husbands of alcoholic women (Ablon, 1976). In addition, the overwhelming number of alcoholics treated by the author have been men, single women (at the time they sought counseling), or alcoholic couples. Discussions with colleagues indicate that some counselors have had to contend with problems presented by husbands of alcoholic women, but the number has been relatively small.

that they are, with justification, very unhappy people. It should then follow that improvement in the alcoholic client should be welcomed by the spouse. However, for *certain* wives this may not be the case.

Variables to Consider
1. the "independent" spouse
2. the "martyred" spouse
3. conjoint vs. separate counseling
4. alcoholic couples

In the study of abnormal behavior it is not uncommon to find an entire family falling apart when one previously disturbed member begins to improve. Many psychiatrists have noted that the stability of a particular family may be based on the need to maintain one member as "insane." All attention, effort, and emotion is directed towards that family member at the expense of any emotional interaction between the others. As the "insane" member improves, the status quo is altered. Unable to cope with the wide range of emotional difficulties that created the need to maintain one member as "insane" in the first place, the family unit virtually collapses. This is, of course, the most extreme result, but in most families a significant change in one member affects all the others to some extent. The degree and direction of the effects seem to depend upon how the family adjusted prior to the change in the "sick" member.

Over the years, the spouse of an alcoholic may have developed a lifestyle of relative independence, perceiving her husband as merely someone to put up with. Or she may be prone to a "martyred" existence, accepting her husband's alcoholism as her burden, and, in order to maintain her own personal stability, accepting life as fraught with problems she must cope with. To a large extent, the continued adjustment of both "independent" and "martyred" wives is based on their husbands' continued drinking. Although they may openly express a strong desire for the husband to quit drinking, even urging him to seek assistance, they harbor the secret, possibly unconscious hope that his alcoholism will continue.

Often the "independent" wife has rejected her husband

sexually, avoids expressions of affection, engages in activities that permit her to leave the house when he is home, and attempts to live in a parallel rather then interactional arrangement with him. When interaction occurs it is either neutral or is a major row — which reinforces her need to avoid all but minimal contact. Such women are unlikely to leave their husbands because their backgrounds often contain a strong religious and moral belief in the institution of marriage as "sacred."

However, a major change in the husband's alcohol consumption is a very real threat to the wife's independence and habits of avoidance. Often through guilt and passivity the alcoholic husband has accepted his wife's behavior, expressing frustration at being ignored only when he is drinking heavily. As a client, he is learning not only how to control his drinking, but also to make a concerted effort to improve his relationship with his wife (something she probably no longer wants). The balance within the marriage has been seriously upset, which may lead to a frantic attempt by the wife to restore the previous equilibrium. In the author's experience the improved alcoholic husband reports either increased rejection and/or gradually deepening depression on the part of his wife.

Under such conditions, it might appear that conjoint treatment should be undertaken. However, at least initially this is not a desirable approach because from the wife's perspective the real "enemy" is her husband's counselor. Although such reasoning is irrational, as the wife may have strongly encouraged her husband to seek assistance, she quite likely holds the counselor responsible for what is happening to her and views the counselor as her husband's ally. Thus, if she is willing to accept help for herself (and out of desperation she may be), a second counselor should be provided. If, as her own treatment proceeds, she concludes that she *is* willing to try to continue with her marriage under the "new rules," conjoint counseling can then be undertaken. Referral to a counselor who has had no previous contact with either spouse would be most appropriate. If this is not possible, the author has experienced good results when both the husband's and wife's counselors conduct the conjoint counseling together.

The "martyred" wife often attempts to elicit sympathy by

119

complaining to friends, relatives, and anyone else who is willing to listen, about the torment she must continually experience, while at the same time expressing that somehow she will endure her fate. Quite commonly she also seeks the support of her children, attempting to drive a wedge between them and their father, and expecting them to appreciate her suffering. Her childhood upbringing may have inculcated a strong and excessively punitive conscience — a prerequisite for martyrdom. She thus derives purpose and meaning for her life by appeasing her conscience through personal suffering. (Although there is no research evidence to support this opinion, the author suspects that such women may well be attracted to men who inadvertently help maintain their suffering.) The attitude of the martyred wife towards her husband is typically ambivalent: her frequent threats to leave when the pain becomes too great — which she may carry out, but usually for a short period — are counterbalanced by her overriding feeling that he needs her. In order for the "he needs me" belief to be maintained, however, the husband must remain sick, i.e. continue with his alcoholism. Yet because his alcoholism, in her unending treadmill, is a sickness that requires help, she often urges him to seek treatment. Her dilemma is: "I need him to be sick, but if he's sick he needs help." She can't win!

Her characteristic response to her husband's improvement is anger. The improved alcoholic client usually reports more arguments at home and frequent negative remarks about the counselor. An interview with the wife to "sort things out" may very well reinforce her "no win" situation; she is obliged to say the appropriate thing ("Of course I want him to get better") while harboring considerable resentment towards the counselor for tampering with her raison d'être by helping her husband to abstain. Without her willingness to receive counseling, the marriage is in imminent danger.

As the "martyred" wife is often an extremely difficult client to work with, her husband's counselor would be a most inappropriate choice. Because her adjustment to life requires suffering, and the sympathy she receives from friends and relatives reinforces it, she is likely to try to enlist the sympathy and support of the counselor as well, with such strong expressions as "I've given him everything and cared for him all these years; now he doesn't need me," or "What have I gotten for all I had to put up with? Nothing!" These angry but often carefully calculated remarks can lead the counselor into a bind. Sympathy is inappropriate, but if it is not forthcoming the "martyr" makes the irrational assumption that the counselor doesn't care, as "care" (for her) means sympathy for her martyrdom. She may also use the counseling sessions to express disbelief that her husband's progress will be maintained — "I've seen him quit a half-dozen times. He's conned that counselor." For her, this attitude must be maintained if her martyrdom is to have a future. The only realistic course of action for the counselor is to empathize rather than sympathize, i.e. to say, "I can see that you feel you are justified in your anger" (an observation *without* support) rather than, "I can understand why you are justified in your anger" (an observation *with* support). But due to the strong need *not* to change, which is a deeply embedded personality trait, the author admits to having had little success with such clients. Conjoint treatment might be attempted with a new counselor, but if the alcoholic client does not return to alcohol, conjoint counseling often ends in separation counseling. Indeed, the infrequent occasions that the author has observed where intervention with the "martyr" has been somewhat successful occurred *after* separation, when the wife has only two real options: seek sympathy for the separation or seek to change herself in order to reestablish the marriage in a different manner.

When both a husband and wife have alcohol problems and seek help, it is incumbent upon the counselor to treat them together. Certain assumptions can usually be made about an alcoholic dyad. Alcohol often serves as a "bridge" between them, and their ability to relate to each other without it is at best difficult. They tend to mutually reinforce each other's drinking behavior, i.e. when one goes to the liquor cabinet the other may be asked, "How about a drink?" Cessation of drinking by one member of the dyad (for whatever reason) tends to produce anxiety and anger in the other, often leading to a major marital crisis. Because alcohol is so much a part of the relationship, conjoint therapy should be undertaken from the beginning, especially if only one expresses a desire to quit or cut down.

22. Wife's Vested Interest

Conjoint treatment often postpones the crisis that results from one spouse's attempt to abstain, because the drinking member is obliged to show at least superficial understanding and support. This "window dressing" is an attempt — sometimes even a self-deceptive attempt — to give the counselor the impression that the drinker agrees with the appropriateness of the spouse's decision. But the crisis will come, and the counselor should be prepared for it. There is simply too much at stake for the spouse who continues to drink: a powerful reinforcer is slipping away, and the continuance of the relationship is threatened.

Another phenomenon for which the counselor should be prepared is blaming. In almost every alcoholic couple with whom the author has worked, very hostile blaming is expressed by the spouse who is trying to quit: "*You* were the drunk in the first place! You dragged me from social drinking into alcoholism!" This may be the first real expression of anger witnessed by the counselor and often it is the first step towards the crisis. The counselor's response must be clear and realistic: "What has occurred in the past cannot be undone. We must concern ourselves with the here and now." But even if the blaming is worked through with the counselor's help, anger is likely to multiply quickly, as the abstaining spouse finds it more and more difficult to live with the continuing drinker, who subtly — and sometimes not so subtly — attempts to undermine the abstainer. The drinking partner, dropping the "window dressing," is most likely to interpret the other's behavior as rejection, even when the abstainer pleads that his or her attempt to quit is in the best interests of both. The "bridge" between them has suffered considerable damage, and communications other than anger are on the verge of breaking down.

Clearly, working with such couples is a challenge. The counselor is in the difficult position of tacitly approving of the partner trying to abstain yet must not appear as an ally of the abstainer. Concern and understanding must be forthcoming for the drinking partner, who is fearful, even panicky, about what seems to be an impending disaster. The counselor must remain neutral, attempting to help both partners explain their own

122

feelings to each other. The continuing drinker will have more difficulty with accurate expression, feeling torn between the "appropriate" thing to say and the unexpressed desire for the abstainer to return to the prior status quo. Role playing may prove helpful; both partners may gain more appreciation for the other's feelings by switching roles.

But whether the "bridge" can be repaired is open to question. Even if the undermining behavior ceases, the abstainer is soberly confronted with the task of relating to the frequently intoxicated partner. Often the abstainer exerts unrelenting pressure on the drinker to quit or dramatically cut down, and if this does not occur the rift widens. The untenable relationship usually produces either a relapse in the abstainer (an attempt to reestablish the bridge) or separation. Without taking sides, the counselor must help the couple recognize the probable outcomes if the drinking partner continues to drink. But while he or she can point out certain realities, the counselor has very little control over the outcome.

Nevertheless, a few strategies can have an impact. The drinking partner's resistance to quitting may not be exclusively due to habituated dependence on alcohol. It is possible that the drinker believes that he or she cannot express affection and relate to the other without alcohol. If explorations with the drinking partner about the reasons for continued consumption indicate that this is the case, the counselor can directly intervene by using the relatively neutral atmosphere of the office to help the couple experiment while both are sober. Early exercises might include making a positive statement about each other, holding hands without verbal communication, and making eye-contact. Although these may appear to be overly simple tasks, they usually have a surprisingly strong emotional impact. The exercises can be practised at home when *both* are sober, and the emotional intensity of the exercises can be increased (e.g. embracing) at a gradual pace until sober affectional behavior occurs spontaneously. Fear of poor sexual performance is typically linked to feelings of inadequacy about other social skills, and often maintains alcohol consumption. Here too, the counselor might be able to intervene effectively. (Sex counseling for alcoholic clients is discussed in

22. Wife's Vested Interest

Miller and Mastria, 1977, pp. 103-124.) It should be kept in mind that work in these areas is likely to prove just as beneficial to the abstaining partner.

Helping the drinking partner to learn, when sober, to express feelings and to act in ways that have previously been supported by alcohol *may* lead to an increased willingness to attempt to abstain. In fact, abstinence by the drinker seems the only possible alternative to relapse by the spouse or separation.

The case in which both partners have made a decision to abstain and jointly seek counseling assistance is not viewed as relevant to this section, as it implies that neither would have a vested interest in maintaining the other's alcoholism.

References

Ablon, J., Family structure and behavior in alcoholism: a review of the literature, in *The Biology of Alcoholism Volume 4 Social Aspects of Alcoholism*, B. Kissen and H. Begleiter (Eds.), 205-242, Plenum Press, 1976.

Alcohol and Drug Problems Association of North America, *National Certification of Non-Professional Alcoholism Counselors: A Report*, Washington, D.C., 1974.

Armor, D.J., Polich, J.M., and Stambul, H.B., *Alcoholism and Treatment*, Rand Corporation, Santa Monica, California, 1976.

Baekeland, F., Lundwall, L., and Kissin, B., Methods of treatment of chronic alcoholism: a critical approach, in *Research Advances in Alcohol and Drug Problems*, Volume II, R.J. Gibbins et al. (Eds.), 247-327, John Wiley and Sons, New York, 1975.

Bandura, A., Lipsher, D.H., and Miller, P.E., Psychotherapists' approach — avoidance reactions to patients' expressions of hostility, *Journal of Consulting Psychology*, 24: 1-8, 1960.

Berkowitz, L., *Aggression: A Social Psychological Analysis*, McGraw-Hill, New York, 1962.

Bowen, W.T. and Twemlow, S.W., Locus of control and treatment dropout in an alcoholic population, *British Journal of Addiction*, 73: 51-54, 1978.

Boyatzis, R.E., The predisposition toward alcohol-related interpersonal aggression in men, *Journal of Studies on Alcohol*, 36: 1196-1207, 1975.

Boylin, R., Gestalt games for alcoholics, *Psychotherapy: Therapy, Research and Practice*, 12: 198-199, 1975.

Bruch, H., *Learning Psychotherapy*, Harvard Press, Cambridge, Mass., 1974.

References

Cahalan, D., Cisin, I.H., and Crossley, H.M., *American Drinking Practices*, Rutgers Center Alcohol Studies, New Brunswick, N.J., 1969.

Catanzaro, R.J., *Alcoholism*, Charles C. Thomas, Springfield, Ill., 1968.

Chafetz, M.E., Addiction III: alcoholism, in *Comprehensive Textbook of Psychiatry*, A.M. Freedman and H.I. Kaplan, (Eds.), 1011-1026, Williams and Wilkins Company, Baltimore, 1967.

Chafetz, M.E., Practical and theoretical considerations in the psychotherapy of alcoholism, *Quarterly Journal of Studies on Alcohol*, 20: 281-291, 1959.

Curlee, J., Attitudes that facilitate or hinder treatment of alcoholism, *Psychotherapy: Theory, Research and Practice*, 8: 65-70, 1971.

Dielthelm, O., *Etiology of Chronic Alcoholism*, Charles C. Thomas, Springfield, Ill., 1955.

Dijk, W.K. van and Dijk-Koffeman, A. van, A follow-up study of 211 treated male alcoholic patients, *British Journal of Addiction*, 68: 3-24, 1973.

Edwards, G.A., The meaning and treatment of alcohol dependence, *British Journal of Hospital Medicine*, 12: 272-277, 1967.

Emrick, C., A review of psychologically oriented treatment of alcoholism, *Journal of Studies on Alcohol*, 36: 88-108, 1975.

Ewalt, J.F., Strecker, E.A., and Ebaugh, F.G. (Eds.), *Practical Clinical Psychiatry*, McGraw-Hill, New York, 1957.

Fitzgerald, F.L., High life among adult chimpanzees, in *Current Trends in Alcoholism*, F.A. Seixas, (Ed.), 265-269, Grune and Stratton, New York, 1977.

Forrest, G.G., *Diagnosis and Treatment of Alcoholism*, Charles C. Thomas, Springfield, Ill., 1975.

Fox, R., Treatment of chronic alcoholism, *The Medical Clinics of North America*, 42: 805-814, 1958.

Gamsky, N.R. and Farwell, G., Counselor verbal behavior as a function of client hostility, *Journal of Counselling Psychology*, 13: 184-190, 1966.

References

Gerard, D.L., Saenger, G., and Wile, R., The abstinent alcoholic, *Archives of General Psychiatry*, 6: 99-111, 1962.

Gerard, D.L. and Saenger, G., *Outpatient Treatment of Alcoholism*, University of Toronto Press, Toronto, 1966.

Gerther, R., Raynes, A.E., and Harris, N., Assessment of attendance and outcome at alcoholism clinic, *Quarterly Journal of Studies on Alcohol*, 34: 955-959, 1973.

Gillies, M., Laverty, S.G., Smart, R.G., and Aharan, C.H., Outcomes in treated alcoholics: patient and treatment characteristics in a one-year follow-up study, *Journal of Alcoholism*, 9: 125-134, 1974.

Glasscote, R.M., Plaut, T.F., Hammersley, D.W., O'Neill, F.J., Chafetz, M.E., and Cumming E., *The Treatment of Alcoholism: A Study of Program and Problems*, Joint Information Service, American Psychiatric Association and National Association for Mental Health, Washington, 1967.

Glasser, W., *Reality Therapy: A New Approach to Psychiatry*, Harper and Row, New York, 1965.

Goldstein, A.P., Heller, K., and Sechrest, L.B., *Psychotherapy and the Psychology of Behavior Change*, John Wiley, New York, 1966.

Haymen, M., *Alcoholism: Mechanism and Management*, Charles C. Thomas, Springfield, Ill., 1966.

Hollingshead, A.B. and Redlich, F.C., *Social Class and Mental Illness*, John Wiley, New York, 1958.

Jacobs, M.R., Assessment of risk and treatment of the suicidal individual, Paper presented at *Lecture/Seminar Series*, Addiction Research Foundation, Toronto, 1975.

Knox, W.J., Attitudes of psychiatrists and psychologists toward alcoholism, *American Journal of Psychiatry*, 127: 1675-1679, 1971.

Knox, W.J. Attitudes of social workers and other professional groups toward alcoholism, *Quarterly Journal of Studies on Alcohol*, 34: 1270-1278, 1973.

Krasnoff, A., Difference between alcoholics who complete or withdraw from treatment, *Journal of Studies on Alcohol*, 37: 1666-1671, 1976.

References

Lambert, D., Difficulties in accepting the diagnosis of alcoholism, Selected papers presented at *The 22nd Annual Meeting of the Alcohol and Drug Problems Association of North America*, 44-45, 1971.

Larkin, E.J., *Treatment of Alcoholism*, Addiction Research Foundation, Toronto, 1974.

Lawrence, F.E., Outpatient management of the alcoholic, *Quarterly Journal of Studies on Alcohol*, 22: 117-128, 1961.

Lemere, F., O'Hollaren, P., and Maxwell, M.A., Motivation in the treatment of alcoholism, *Quarterly Journal of Studies on Alcohol*, 19: 428-432, 1958.

Lowe, W.C. and Thomas, S.D., Assessing alcoholism treatment effectiveness: a comparison of three evaluative measures, *Journal of Studies on Alcoholism*, 37: 883-889, 1976.

Lynn, E.J., Treatment for alcoholism: psychotherapy is still alive and well, *Journal of Hospital and Community Psychiatry*, 27: 282-283, 1966.

Madden, J.S., A program of group counselling for alcoholics, in *Alcoholism and Drug Dependence*, J.S. Madden et al., 309-319, Plenum Press, New York, 1976.

Marlatt, G.A., A comparison of aversive conditioning procedures in the treatment of alcoholism, (unpublished paper), Cited in Miller and Mastria, 8, 1977.

Mayer, J. and Myerson, D.J., Outpatient treatment of alcoholics, *Quarterly Journal of Studies on Alcohol*, 32: 620-627, 1971.

Mayfield, D., Alcoholism, alcohol intoxication, and assaultive behavior, *Diseases of the Nervous System*, 27: 288-291, 1976.

Mendelson, J.H., *Alcoholism*, Little, Brown Co., Boston, 1966.

Miller, P. and Mastria, M., *Alternatives to Alcohol Abuse: A Social Learning Model*, Research Press Company, Champaign, Ill., 1977.

Milt, H., *Basic Handbook on Alcoholism*, Scientific Aids Publications, Maplewood, N.J., 1967.

Moberg, P., Clients' subjective view of treatment in an alcoholism clinic, *Alcoholism Digest*, 4: 14-18, 1975.

Moore, R.A., The psychotherapeutics of alcoholism, in *Proceedings of the Second Annual Alcoholism Conference of the National Institute on Alcoholism Abuse and Alcoholism*, M.E. Chafetz (Ed.), 222-233, 1972.

Moore, R.A., Alcoholism treatment in private psychiatric hospitals, *Quarterly Journal of Studies on Alcoholism*, 32: 1038-1045, 1971.

Moore, R.A., Some countertransference reactions in the treatment of alcoholism, *Psychiatry Digest*, 26: 35-43, 1965.

Moore, R.A., The alcoholic versus the healer: a study of noncommunication, *International Psychiatric Clinics*, 1: 107-122, 1964.

Moore, R.A. and Buchanan, T.K., State hospitals and alcoholism: a nationwide survey of treatment techniques and results, Paper presented at the 20th Annual Meeting of the American Psychiatric Association, Los Angeles, 1964.

Murray, E.J. and Jacobson, L.I., The nature of learning in traditional and behavioral psychotherapy in *Handbook of Psychotherapy and Behavior Change: An Empirical Analysis*, A.E. Bergin and S.L. Garfield (Eds.), 709-747, John Wiley and Sons, Inc., New York, 1971.

O'Leary, M.R., Rohsenow, D.J., Schau, E.J., and Donovan, D.M., Defensive style and treatment outcome among men alcoholics, *Journal of Studies on Alcohol*, 38: 1036-1040, 1977.

Panepinto, W.C. and Higgins, M.J., Keeping alcoholics in treatment: effective follow-through procedures, *Quarterly Journal of Studies on Alcohol*, 30: 414-419, 1969.

Pittman, D.J. and Sterne, M.W., A concept of motivation — a source of institutional blockage in the treatment of alcoholics, *Quarterly Journal of Studies on Alcohol*, 26: 41-57, 1965.

Redlich, F. and Kellert, S.R., Trends in American mental health, *American Journal of Psychiatry*, 135: 22-28, 1978.

Riessman, F., Cohen, J., and Pearl, A., *Mental Health of the Poor*, Free Press of Glencoe, London, 1964.

References

Roebuck, J.B. and Kessler, R.G., *Etiology of Alcoholism,* Charles C. Thomas, Springfield, Ill., 1972.

Rogers, C., The necessary and sufficient conditions of therapeutic personality change, *Journal of Consulting Psychology,* 21: 95-103, 1957.

Schmidt, W., Smart, R.G., and Moss, M.K., *Social Class and the Treatment of Alcoholism,* University of Toronto Press, Toronto, 1968.

Selzer, M., Hostility as a barrier to therapy in alcoholism, *Psychiatric Quarterly,* 31: 300-305, 1957.

Steiner, C.M., The alcoholic game, *Quarterly Journal of Studies on Alcohol,* 30: 920-938, 1969.

Strupp, H.H., *Psychotherapy and the Modification of Abnormal Behavior,* McGraw-Hill, New York, 1971.

Tamerin, J. and Neuman, C., Psychological aspects of treating alcoholism, *Alcohol Health and Research World,* 2: 14-18, 1974.

Trice, H.M., *Alcoholism in America,* McGraw-Hill, New York, 1966.

Truax, C.B. and Carkhuff, R.R., *Toward Effective Counseling and Psychotherapy,* Adline Publishing Company, Chicago, 1967.

Truax, C.B. and Mitchell, K.M., Research on certain therapist interpersonal skills in relation to process and outcome, in *Handbook of Psychotherapy and Behavior Change,* A.E. Bergin and S.L. Garfield (Eds.), 298-344, John Wiley, New York, 1971.

Vallance, M., Alcoholism: a two-year study of patients admitted to a psychiatric department of a general hospital, *British Journal of Psychiatry III,* 1965: 348-356.

Weiner, I.B., *Principles of Psychotherapy,* John Wiley, New York, 1975.

Wilkinson, A.E., Prado, W.M., Williams, W.O., and Schnadt, F.W., Psychological test characteristics and length of stay in alcoholism treatment, *Quarterly Journal of Studies on Alcohol,* 32: 60-65, 1971.

Wilson, G.R., The management of the alcoholic, *Medical Journal of Australia,* 2: 875-884, 1968.

Wolberg, L.R., *Technique of Psychotherapy, Volume II,* Grune and Stratton, New York, 1967.

Wrightsman, L.S., *Social Psychology of The Seventies,* Brooks/Cole Publishing Company, Monterey, Ca., 1972.